WINGS OF NIGHT SKY ‖ WINGS OF MORNING LIGHT

Joy Harjo with Priscilla Page

WINGS OF NIGHT SKY,

WINGS OF MORNING

LIGHT

|| A Play by Joy Harjo and a Circle of Responses ||

Wesleyan University Press   Middletown, Connecticut

Wesleyan University Press
Middletown CT 06459
www.wesleyan.edu/wespress
© 2019 Joy Harjo and Priscilla Page
All rights reserved
Manufactured in the United States of America
Designed by Mindy Basinger Hill
Typeset in Minion Pro

Library of Congress Cataloging-in-Publication
Data available upon request

Hardcover ISBN: 978-0-8195-7865-5
Paperback ISBN: 978-0-8195-7866-2
Ebook ISBN: 978-0-8195-7867-9

5   4   3   2   1

CONTENTS

Joy Harjo's *Wings*: A Revolution on the American Stage
MARY KATHRYN NAGLE || 1

Wings of Night Sky, Wings of Morning Light: A Ceremony
JOY HARJO || 11

Reflections on Joy Harjo, Indigenous Feminism,
and Experiments in Creative Expression
PRISCILLA PAGE || 42

Toward the Production of New Native Theater:
An Interview with Randy Reinholz
PRISCILLA PAGE || 59

Imagining a Contemporary Native Theater:
An Interview with Rolland Meinholtz
PRISCILLA PAGE || 69

Learning to Be: An Interview with Joy Harjo
PRISCILLA PAGE || 94

Acknowledgments || 105

Contributors || 107

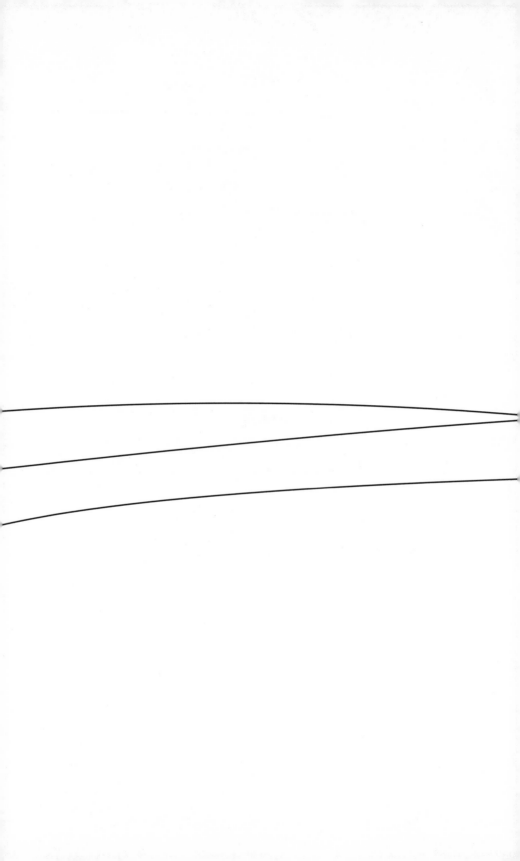

WINGS OF NIGHT SKY ‖ WINGS OF MORNING LIGHT

MARY KATHRYN NAGLE

Joy Harjo's *Wings* || A Revolution on the American Stage

In my family's blue-sky memory, we loved my father without question.
We loved his laugh, his stories, his swinging us through the sky.
We struggled with his fight, his jab, and his fear. When I looked through my
dreaming eyes, he was still a boy of four standing by his mother's casket.
She was his beloved grandfather's great-great-granddaughter. She liked to
paint, blew saxophone in Indian territory and traveled about on Indian
oil money. Still, grief from history grew in her lungs. She was dead of
tuberculosis by her twenties. The grief had to go somewhere.
We had no one left in our family who knew how to bury it.
So it climbed onto her little boy's back.

Joy Harjo, *Wings of Night Sky, Wings of Morning Light*

For too long our grief has had nowhere to go. So we carry it in our lungs. We bury it in our kidneys. It cakes our hearts. We deposit it onto the backs of our children, and our children's children.

We know our stories are medicine. We know they bring about healing. But we have not been permitted to share them. At this point in history, the American stage has, for the most part, silenced the voice of Native artists.

Wings of Night Sky, Wings of Morning Light is exceptional. It is an extraordinary work of extraordinary magnitude for several reasons, but one of its most unique, rare attributes is that it has been presented on a professional American stage. *Wings* constitutes one of but a small handful of Native plays to have ever been presented on such a stage. For me and the other Native playwrights in my generation, *Wings* stands as a source of inspiration. The impossible is possible. And now, with the publication of *Wings*, my hope and prayer is that Americans will come to see that our stories truly are worth reading and staging, and thus for our Native writers, worth writing.

For the generations and generations of American Indians who have never heard or seen a performance by a Native woman on a professional American stage, Joy Harjo's *Wings of Night Sky, Wings of Morning Light* offers a powerful healing. Harjo's heroine Redbird takes her audience on a journey through generations of trauma and survival in a musical revelry that celebrates American Indian resistance. For those of us still attempting to make sense of the trauma lodged in our hearts, *Wings* creates a release valve. Through ceremony, song, and kinship, a public space is created where healing can collectively take place and grief can be processed.

For the generations and generations of non-Natives who have been taught that American Indians are nothing more than the image on the back of a Washington, DC, football jersey, *Wings* commands a powerful reckoning. *Wings* introduces non-Native audience members to what will be, for many, their first interaction with an actual Native person.

Redbird's journey is breathtakingly personal. Of course, when it comes to putting Indians on the American stage, the personal is political. Today, statistics reveal that Americans who go to the theater are more likely to witness the performance of redface onstage than the performance of Native stories by Native people. As a Muscogee Creek woman created by a Muscogee Creek playwright, Redbird is everything her contemporary redface counterparts in *Bloody Bloody Andrew Jackson*, *An Octaroon*, and the Wooster Group's *Cry, Trojans!* (to name a few) are not. Instead of a costume, a drunk Indian who only grunts onstage, a joke, or a stereotype, Redbird is an articulate Native woman with something intelligent—indeed profound—to say about the attempted destruction of her people and sovereign Tribal Government.

We need to see more Redbirds on the American stage. I lived and wrote plays in New York for five years. I found the entire experience rather depressing. During my five years in New York, I witnessed numerous performances of redface on many of New York's most prestigious stages. Not once—in all of my five years—did I ever see a non-Native professional theater company produce a full-length play by a Native playwright. Indeed, I arrived three years after the Public Theater workshopped Harjo's *Wings*, but they never fully produced it. I am encouraged that this publication of *Wings* will allow other theaters to now follow the artistic lead of Randy Reinholz and Jean Bruce Scott, co-creators of Native Voices at the Autry, who premiered the work in 2009 in Los Angeles. This is an important play that openly raises consciousness and exposes truths. I know we are ready for more productions.

To be clear, the absence of authentic Native representation on the America stage is no accident. Redface was purposefully created to tell a false, demeaning story. Redface constitutes a false portrayal of Native people—most often performed by non-Natives wearing a stereotypical "native" costume that bears no relation to actual Native people, our stories, our struggles, or our survival in a country that has attempted to eradicate us. The continued dominant perception that American Indians are the racial stereotypes they see performed on the American stage is devastating to our sovereign right to define our own identity. Of course, that's why it was invented.

In the 185 years since Andrew Jackson drafted and signed into law his Indian Removal Act, portrayals of Native Americans in the American theater have changed very little. The redface performances that originated at the time of removal continue to dominate the American stage today, but for the first time, *now*, we have the opportunity to change the narrative. We have the opportunity to replace a false representation with a real one.

In this respect, Harjo's placement of an articulate, brilliant, and musical Native woman front and center on the American stage constitutes nothing less than an act of revolution. *Wings* is a magnificent rebellion. Redbird's narrative demonstrates defiance.

In contrast to the majority of contemporary Native representations onstage, the Native protagonist in *Wings* does not grunt incoherent sounds, nor does she portray the loss of her Muscogee ancestral homelands as a joke in a modern day rock musical. Instead, the reality of the Trail of Tears is introduced as a shared communal experience of survival, an experience that continues to shape the journey and identity of Muscogee Creek Nation citizens today. Harjo writes,

CEHOTOSAKVTES
CHENAORAKVTES MOMIS KOMET
AWATCHKEN OHAPEYAKARES HVLWEN

Two beloved women sang this song on the trail of tears. One walked near the front of the people, one near the back. When either began to falter, they would sing the song to hold each other up.

DO NOT GET TIRED.
DON'T BE DISCOURAGED. BE DETERMINED, TO ALL
COME IN. WE WILL GO TO THE HIGHEST PLACE.
WE WILL GO TOGETHER. (22)

The power of Harjo's portrayal of the Trail of Tears is not that Andrew Jackson is transformed from hero into villain (as one might imagine a Native playwright would want to do), but rather, the power comes from the fact that both Jackson's presence and his voice are erased entirely. In *Wings*, Andrew Jackson's voice is replaced with the voice of Redbird. Indeed, the only mention of Andrew Jackson in this Muscogee story comes in a few short lines on page 27:

> Don't ever forget the Battle of Horseshoe Bend, said my father. Andrew Jackson's forces killed almost everyone as we stood to protect our lands. Your grandfather Monahwee was shot seven times and still survived.

The power of this replacement cannot be underestimated. In the United States today, Andrew Jackson continues to be celebrated as a hero. His face adorns the most common form of our currency, the twenty-dollar bill, and he is characterized as the sexy protagonist hero of a modern-day rock musical that has been performed on American stages from Broadway to hundreds of colleges and high schools across the nation. In classrooms across the United States, school children study all of the "wonderful" things that Andrew Jackson did to ensure American democracy. Or as David Greenberg claimed, writing for *Politico Magazine* in summer 2015, Jackson is "the president who made American democracy democratic."

As a citizen of Cherokee Nation, and as a direct descendant of Cherokee leaders who fought—and won—the right to continued tribal sovereignty in the United States Supreme Court (*Wooster v. Georgia*), I know all too well the price we pay for celebrating the "legacy" of the only president in United States history to openly defy an order from the Supreme Court. In 1832, just nine years after the Supreme Court declared Indians incapable of claiming legal title to their own land because they constitute "an inferior race" in *Johnson v. M'Intosh*, Justice Marshall issued a ruling declaring that the State of Georgia could not exercise jurisdiction on Cherokee lands because Cherokee Nation is a sovereign, "distinct community, occupying its own territory" with "the preexisting power of the Nation to govern itself." Following this victory, my grandfather John Ridge visited President Jackson in the White House. My grandfather asked how the federal government would enforce the Supreme Court's decision. Andrew Jackson told him, "John Marshall has issued his decision. Let him enforce it." And with the turn of his hand, Andrew Jackson became the only president in the history of the United States to refuse to enforce an order from the Supreme Court.

Jackson not only defied the Supreme Court—he also violated the plain text of congressional statutes that he himself signed into law. In 1830, Jackson signed the Indian Removal Act, the plain language of which required a removal treaty with an Indian Nation before its citizens could be moved. However, as Suzan Shown Harjo points out in her 2015 article for *HowlRound*, "Andrew Jackson Is Not as Bad as You Think, He's Far, Far Bloodier," Jackson never negotiated or signed a removal treaty with the Muscogee Creek Nations; instead, there "was no removal treaty and removal was carried out at bayonet point . . . Tens of millions of acres were taken illegally, and the Muscogee Peoples still grieve over the displacement, ill treatment, and injustice, and for the homelands and ancestors left behind."

The substitution of the voice of a Muscogee woman for that of Andrew Jackson in *Wings* constitutes a significant, and laudable, departure from the traditional American theater cannon. *Wings* does not offer lengthy exposition, nor does it purport to educate the audience on all of the events in American history that their grade school educators failed to teach them. Instead, *Wings* offers what nearly all contemporary American theaters refuse to show: an honest, authentic portrayal of an American Indian woman's journey in the twenty-first century. The fact that *Wings'* protagonist happens to be a direct descendant of the people Jackson violently and forcibly removed on a Trail of Tears renders Harjo's work a powerful contrast to the majority of redface being performed on the American stage today. Harjo's presentation of story and character is delivered in such an artistic way that, as audience members, we cannot help but gulp in her words breath by breath. With each inhale comes human experience, and with each exhale, we bid farewell to a now useless stereotype.

Harjo's *Wings* redefines the American Indian experience from the Andrew Jackson removal era to the boarding school era to today. We now find ourselves fighting to restore the sovereignty of our Tribal Governments, the authenticity of our stories, and ultimately, the right to define our identity. And nowhere is this fight more critical than in the lives of our Indian women. Today, on the American stage, in Hollywood, and in Halloween costume shops across the United States, Native women are portrayed as nothing more than objects to be conquered sexually. From "Pocahottie" costumes to Disney's *Pocahontas*, the message is clear: Native women are not to be respected—they are to be exploited.

As a Cherokee woman, and as an attorney, I cannot separate the high rates of violence against our women from the artistic expressions that dominate American society portraying Native women as sexual victims with no agency or power. And we are exploited more so than any other group in the entire United States.

Today, reports from the United States Department of Justice (DOJ) reveal that Native women are more likely to be battered, raped, or sexually assaulted than any other US population. One in three Native women will be raped in her lifetime, and six in ten will be physically assaulted. On some reservations, the murder rate for Native women is ten times the national average. Native children suffer similar rates of trauma and sexual abuse, as their rates of violent victimization ranks 2.5 times higher than the national average for all other children.

Wings offers an alternative narrative. Redbird's examination of the violence in her community is inextricably linked to the intergenerational trauma her family has suffered since forced removal. *Wings* makes clear that violence against Native women in tribal communities is the continuation of a cycle of trauma and grief that began with the Trail of Tears, and, unfortunately, has not yet been allowed to conclude, in large part because we have not been permitted to honestly discuss it on the American stage and in society at large.

In a nation that has instructed Native women to remain silent, *Wings* signals to Native women that it is permissible for them to publicly share their stories of survival. Through Redbird's memories, the audience bears witnesses to the violence that erupts from Redbird's father when he is triggered:

After my mother sang, she and my father fought.
Their friends scattered.
I tried to pull him off her, and he went crazy.
He threw me across the room into the wall.
What happened to the storytelling father? Where did the man go who made
  my mother laugh? (*Wings*, 28)

Wings does not shift responsibility away from individual perpetrators of violence against Native women. Instead, Redbird's story reveals that the perpetuation of this violence is only made possible through the silencing of Native survivors. Currently, the majority of American plays portray violence against Native people as a joke, and as a result, non-Natives have no context in which they have learned to take violence against Native women seriously. And because American culture promotes the sexual commodification of Native women, the violence perpetrated against our women in our own homes is overlooked; in most instances, it simply goes unnoticed. Redbird's sharing of the violence she and her mother have endured forces the American audience to consider a reality they have been previously told to ignore.

Wings could not come forward for publication at a time more critical in relation to the national movement to restore safety for Native women. Today, the majority of violent assaults committed against American Indians are committed by non-Indians. In fact, a 1999 report from the Bureau of Justice found that "[a]t least 70 percent of the violent victimizations experienced by American Indians are committed by persons not of the same race" (Greenfield and Smith, iv). In cases of sexual assault, research has shown that 67 percent of the perpetrators are non-Native. Thus, although historical trauma has introduced rape to our Native men who now abuse our women, our women are more likely to suffer abuse in the hands of a non-Native—someone who has learned that such abuse will be tolerated as a result of the objectification of Native women he has witnessed in American culture and society at large.

Wings does not shy away from the prevalence of non-Indian violence on Native women and children. Following the departure of Redbird's biological Muscogee father, Redbird describes the series of suitors who entered their home, desiring her mother, including several non-Indian men who abuse Redbird, her mother, and her siblings:

> A preacher dressed in black planned to save us with a lash. He had God on his
>   side. Get down on your knees and pray for the sins of your divorced Indian
>   mother, your Indian father, he hissed behind her back.
> We helped our mother push him and his angry God out the door. (31)

In this regard, *Wings* touches on what has become an epidemic of non-Indian violence perpetrated against Indian women in tribal communities. It is no coincidence that Harjo graduated from Iowa Writers' Workshop in 1978. That was the same year the United States Supreme Court decided *Oliphant v. Suquamish Indian Tribe*, where they declared that American Indian Nations no longer "have criminal jurisdiction over non-Indians" who commit crimes on tribal lands. The Supreme Court in *Oliphant* based its decision on an earlier precedent, established in the 1823 case *Johnson v. M'Intosh*, that "the power to dispose of the soil at their own will, to whomsoever they pleased was inherently lost to the overriding sovereignty of the United States" (*Oliphant*, 209, quoting *Johnson v. M'Intosh*, 8).

The Supreme Court in *Johnson v. M'Intosh* was clear. Indian tribes lost this power to dispose of their own land and could not retain title over their land because the court considered them to be "savages" and "an inferior race of people, without the privileges of citizens, and under the perpetual protection and pupilage of the government." The court's decision in 1823 that Indians are racially inferior and savages has never been overturned or declared unconstitutional. Instead, it remains the legal basis for the Supreme Court's continued denial of tribal sovereignty and jurisdiction to protect Native women today.

Following the Supreme Court's 1978 decision in *Oliphant*, rates of non-Indian violence against Native women skyrocketed. Suddenly, non-Indian men realized they could move onto tribal lands and rape, murder, or abuse Native women, and there was nothing her Tribal Government could do to protect her or prosecute him. Having graduated from Iowa in 1978, Harjo commenced her creative career at a time when the harmful, false narrative of American Indian identity reached its climax—resulting in the legal stripping of our tribes' inherent right to protect Native women from abuse and sexual violence. In this regard, *Wings* constitutes a much-needed response to the absence of the voices of Native women, both in the United States Supreme Court and on the American stage.

It is alarming that the same redface performances created to justify the Supreme Court's decision in *Johnson v. M'Intosh* remain alive and well on the American stage today. It should come as no surprise, then, that the laws redface helped to shape and create continue to control the lives of American Indians today. For Native women, this reality of redface is devastating.

We know stories are medicine. We know they are healing. We know that when violence is discussed out in the open—and not hidden behind a costume or celebrated in a sexy rock musical—hearts and minds will change. And we know that when hearts and minds change, laws change. And when laws change, lives are saved.

But laws will never change if the stories we tell remain the same. Without a doubt, the United States remains stuck in a nineteenth-century colonial legal framework. What does it mean when, in twenty-first-century America, the United States Supreme Court still classifies our people as "racially inferior"? It means we have to tell our stories. Stories and performances were constructed to allow the Supreme Court to conclude that we are "racially inferior"—stories that continue to find their way to the American stage today. The only way to deconstruct a falsely fabricated prejudicial story is to tell a real one.

Wings is a real story. I do not mean to infer that it is autobiographical, because it is not. Joy Harjo is not Redbird. But Harjo and Redbird are constructed from the same fabric, the same experience, the same survival. Redbird's stories, her words, her perspective, are all derived from the perspective that playwright Joy

Harjo holds as a Muscogee Creek/Cherokee woman. It is a perspective that only a Muscogee Creek/Cherokee woman can know.

Wings offers a healing not only to Native people, but to non-Natives as well. The play itself takes the form of a collective, indigenous ceremony. Indeed, the play's opening lines welcome the audience to a ceremony: "I welcome you on behalf of the family, and thank you so much for coming out to help with our ceremony" (20).

Redbird clarifies for the non-Native audience that the performance they are about to witness is more than a play; it is ceremony. Ceremony is inherently a collective experience. Healing takes place in ceremony. And in many tribal communities, healing ceremonies involve expressive communications. Grief, shame, despair—a range of emotions may be shared, lessening the burden and trauma for all. Whether in the form of prayer or shared story, the shared communication between community members enables healing. It is no coincidence, then, that after the sharing of the Trail of Tears song, at the front of the play, Redbird announces, "Now, our ceremony begins" (22).

Following the commencement of the *ceremony*, the testimonials are shared. Redbird shares her story—and at its conclusion, she returns to one of the most fundamental aspects of many Native ceremonies: the giveaway. At the conclusion of *Wings*, Harjo writes on page 48:

(REDBIRD appears on stage carrying a basket of food and goods.)

Spirit Helper brought me home again to this table. Everything you need for your healing is here, she told me.
The table is within you; it has always been within you. You must remember to acknowledge the gifts. "You must remember to share," she said. Then she gave me her shawl.
This giveaway is in honor of our ceremony tonight, in honor of all the gifts of struggle of every one of us here.

(Gifts are shared with the audience in this traditional giveaway.)

The giveaway at the conclusion of *Wings* stands in stark contrast to the culture of mainstream American theater, where audience members come to the theater to give to the artist, and not the other way around. That is, in American theater, audience members pay the artist money and expect to receive nothing in return, except perhaps some entertainment or laughter. In this regard, theater is treated as a commodity.

But in *Wings*, theater is a gift. The story is a gift. It is a shared experience through which both performer and audience members leave the play with a remarkable benefit. It is a benefit that cannot be quantified in monetary terms, but rather, is made evident in the creation of community and a public space where authentic identity may be expressed, and ultimately accepted.

I never got to see the 2007 workshop of *Wings* at the Public Theater, but I certainly heard about it. And it inspired me. Suddenly the impossible felt possible. Instead of characters that wear fake feathers and grunt onstage, one of America's most prestigious theaters had agreed to workshop and present a play that portrays my people, Native people, as human.

Wings offers something true. Something powerful. I hope some non-Native theater companies agree to share it.

WORKS CITED

Elk v. Wilkins. 112. US Supreme Court. 1884. Online.

Greenberg, David. "Keep Andrew Jackson on the $20." *Politico*, June 14, 2015. Available at www.politico.com/. Accessed January 5, 2017.

Greenfield, Lawrence A., and Steven K. Smith. United States, Department of Justice, Office of Justice Programs, Bureau of Justice Statistics. American Indians and Crime BJS Statisticians, February 1999, NCJ 173386.

Harjo, Joy. "Wings of Night Sky, Wings of Morning Light." Unpublished. Permission of the author, 2014.

Harjo, Suzan Shown. "Andrew Jackson Is Not as Bad as You Think, He's Far, Far Bloodier." *Howlround*, February 26, 2015. Available at howlround.com/. Accessed December 22, 2016.

Johnson v. M'Intosh. 543. US Supreme Court. 1823. Online.

Lone Wolf v. Hitchcock. 275. US Supreme Court. 1903. Online.

Oliphant v. Suquamish Indian Tribe. 435. US Supreme Court. 1978. Online.

United States v. Sandoval. 231. US Supreme Court. 1913. Online.

Wooster v. Georgia. 515. US Supreme Court. 1832. Online.

JOY HARJO

Wings of Night Sky, Wings of
Morning Light || A Ceremony

Wings of Night Sky, Wings of Morning Light
by Joy Harjo (Mvskoke) ||
Development and Production History

DECEMBER 2007
Public Theater Native
Theater Festival
New York, New York
Workshop and Staged Reading

JUNE 2008
Native Voices at the
Autry Playwrights Retreat
and Festival of New Plays
San Diego and
Los Angeles, California
Workshop and Staged Reading

MARCH 2009
Native Voices at the Autry
Los Angeles, California
Equity World Premiere

JANUARY 2010
Alaska Native Heritage Center
Anchorage, Alaska
Tour

MARCH 2010
Merrimack College
North Andover, Massachusetts
Tour

MAY 2010
Outpost Performance Space
Albuquerque, New Mexico
Tour

JUNE 2010
Native Voices at the Autry Festival
of New Plays
La Jolla, California
Tour

SEPTEMBER 2010
Oklahoma Center for Poets and
Writers, Tulsa Library Trust,
American Indian Resource Center,
and Readers' Library
Tulsa, Oklahoma
Tour

DECEMBER 2010
Native Voices at the Autry with the
Public Theater
New York, New York
Workshop

OCTOBER 2011
University of Massachusetts
Amherst, Massachusetts
Reading

February 2012
First Nations House of Learning
University of British Columbia,
Vancouver, BC, Canada
Performance

CHARACTERS

REDBIRD, who may also be the SPIRIT HELPER: a Native woman, Mvskoke, somewhere in her later twenties, thirties, forties, or fifties

GUARDIAN MUSICIAN: a guitar player who accompanies Redbird on her journey

> *GUARDIAN MUSICIAN comes onstage about five minutes before the curtain speech to set up gear and tune as needed. He sits extreme stage right.*

OPENING

> *GUARDIAN MUSICIAN plays funky music. Music accompanies the story throughout.*
> *The kitchen table, stage left center, is the gut around which all action flows. It is a heart, a bed, a bier, a car, a counter at the bar, an altar, and a hiding place.*
> *Lights up on the table.*
> *REDBIRD enters upstage left, lands down center stage. She wears jeans, red shirt, and cowboy boots.*
> *Light bright sunlight.*

REDBIRD: I welcome you on behalf of the family, and thank you so much for coming out to help with our ceremony. Important information: The bathrooms are down the hall, and there's water and coffee in the kitchen. Don't forget to turn off your cell phones, iPads, cameras . . . no taping, or texting.

> *REDBIRD, as REDBIRD'S relative, picks up rattle and shakes it.*

REDBIRD: Please keep in mind that the patient Redbird Monahwee is in a delicate and vulnerable state. There is imbalance between dark and light. We need your good thoughts to help see us through.
And here to assist us in our ceremony is Redbird's protector guardian.

> *GUARDIAN MUSICIAN plays a flourish on guitar as a way of introduction. He never speaks in the play.*

REDBIRD: I've been asked to open with a traditional family story and song, so that our minds come together as one.

Mvto, mvto, thank you: for ancestral and all spiritual help.

REDBIRD shakes a rattle to signal the beginning of the story.

SONG: RABBIT IS UP TO TRICKS

In a world long before this one, there was enough for everyone
until somebody got out of line.
We heard it was Rabbit, fooling around with clay and the wind.
Everybody was tired of his tricks and no one would play with him;
he was lonely in this world.
So Rabbit thought to make a person.
And when he blew into the mouth of that crude figure
to see what would happen, the clay man stood up.
Rabbit showed the clay man how to *steal* a chicken.
The clay man obeyed.
Then Rabbit showed him how to *steal* corn.
The clay man obeyed.
Then he showed him how to *steal* someone else's wife.
The clay man obeyed.
Rabbit *felt* important and powerful.
The clay man *felt* important and powerful.
And once that clay man started he could not stop.
Once he took that chicken he wanted all the chickens.
And once he took that corn he wanted all the corn.
And once he took that wife, he wanted all the wives.
He was insatiable.
Then he had a taste of gold and he wanted all the gold.
Then it was land and anything else he saw.
His wanting only made him want more.
Soon it was countries, and then it was trade.
The wanting infected the earth.
We lost track of the purpose and reason for life.
We began to forget our songs, our stories;

we could no longer see or hear our ancestors,
or talk with each other across the kitchen table.
Forests were being mowed down all over the world to make more.
And Rabbit had no place to play.
Rabbit's trick had backfired.
Rabbit tried to call the clay man back,
But when the clay man wouldn't listen
Rabbit realized he'd made a clay man with no ears.

SONG: WINDING THROUGH THE MILKY WAY

CEHOTOSAKVTES
CHENAORAKVTES MOMIS KOMET
AWATCHKEN OHAPEYAKARES HVLWEN

REDBIRD: Two beloved women sang this song on the trail of tears. One walked near the front of the people, one near the back. When either began to falter, they would sing the song to hold each other up.

DO NOT GET TIRED.
DON'T BE DISCOURAGED. BE DETERMINED,
TO ALL COME IN. WE WILL GO TO THE HIGHEST PLACE.
WE WILL GO TOGETHER.

Rattle ends the song.

REDBIRD: Now, our ceremony begins.

SCENE 1

Light bright day.
Light up on kitchen table.

REDBIRD: It was at this kitchen table I was forbidden to sing when I was fourteen. I wasn't the best singer. It wasn't about that at all.

The man who had made himself keeper of our house stood there with my
   stack of albums in his hands.
I had bought and paid for them with money from my dishwashing job. The
   music was my comfort, my joy.

REDBIRD dances and sings. Sings first, then plays horn.

I sang, and when I sang I felt all sorrow, all sadness fall away. I could fly far
   away with my singing wings.

REDBIRD ends with sax riff.

This is what I think about your singing, he shouted, as he broke my albums:
There will be no more singing in this house.
When I come back from a day's work, I need peace and quiet. And if you tell
   your mother,
I will break the both of you as easily as I have broken your silly music.
Some of my light was put out then.
I walked away and left part of myself behind.
"This is where it begins," I told Spirit Helper as we sat at her kitchen table.
She asked me, "Redbird, why are you here?"
My father is wandering drunk about the earth, and
my mother was stolen by a heartless keeper.
"Why are you here?"
My son is lost in a cloud of drink.
My daughter is in the streets of the city.
"Why are you here?"
I'm here, because I have lost my way.
"Okay, then I think I can help you," she said.
"If we make the right tracks, we will find the lost pieces of your soul."
Then Spirit Helper called in the guardians to open the door.

REDBIRD as SPIRIT HELPER. She chants.

We call in the guardians of the night sky.
We call in the guardians of morning light.
We call in the guardians of falling apart.

We call in the guardians of making right.

We call in the memory keepers, those who have kept the songs of the earthly soul.

We call in the keepers of peace, though they be heavy with the witness of war.

We stand here respectfully at the edge of our small world and ask for help from the shining ones who have gone before.

REDBIRD: *(to the audience)* After she called in the guardians, Spirit Helper told me, "Redbird, we have to return to the beginning of the story if we are to find all the pieces."

SCENE 2

Light bright day.

REDBIRD: When my spirit crossed worlds to join my father and mother, there were no songs to assist the birth.

There was no cedar or tobacco . . . but—my mother had drugs!

My body was a wet, ripe, bloody seed

And it was about to be spit onto the red earth of Oklahoma.

That's when I changed my mind.

My mother's body pushed. I pushed back.

We struggled. I panicked.

It was then that Spirit Helper lifted me to see my laboring mother-to-be. She was just a girl, a beautiful Cherokee waitress who was so in love with my father-to-be, a good-looking Creek man who was puffing away on a Lucky Strike outside the waiting room.

But, but I heard myself stutter: I don't want this world at all.

It was then I heard the voice of the Spirit Helper: "You will forget everything."

"But I won't forget," I argued.

BABY cries.

And then, I did.

SCENE 3

Light night.

REDBIRD: They partied every Friday night after payday.
My father brought home his buddies and their supplies from the bootlegger
    next door.
My mother cooked fried chicken, mashed potatoes and gravy.
She partied with them, I heard her tell her best friends, from my perch under
    the kitchen table:
If you can't fight them, join them.
It was fun. We kids ate, ran around in the yard in our pajamas.
My father would smile as his work fell away from him.
He pulled my mother to his lap.
I can still hear her laugh as she slid away to set the table with her girlfriends.
Later they'd turn the lights down and we'd all jitterbug and twist together.

REDBIRD dances.

My father would tell old stories. I liked the one best about his great-great-
    grandfather Monahwee and his favorite horse. He and his fast black horse
    could beat anyone in a race.
My great-great-grandfather always had the best horse, said my father. He was a
    sharp horse trader, and could even speak with horses in their own language.
And not only that, old Monahwee knew how to bend time.
What do you mean, bend time? I always asked.
Time is a being, like you and me.
No one pays much attention, until they're sad, then time stops.
Or when they're having fun running around in their pajamas and it is time to
    go to bed, there isn't enough time.
His eyes would shine for me.
Monahwee made friends with time, shared tobacco with time. So when he
    got on his horse to race his beloved warrior friends, he had a little talk with
    time. Time said, "Get on my back and we'll fly free."
So, no matter how fast all the others raced, Monahwee and his horse arrived
    long before it was possible, little Redbird.
Those were the best times, said my father.

Those were the best times. And when my father and his friends were drinking, they were always followed by the worst times.

My truck is my horse, he laughed.

The only race I have is outrunning the Whiteman.

His friends laughed. My mother flinched. She knew he was winding up.

What happened to Monahwee, I asked?

My father told me to "open me another beer, honey."

I liked thinking about the person of time.

I liked thinking about my father on the back of a horse, carried by the wings of time.

Don't ever forget the Battle of Horseshoe Bend, said my father. Andrew Jackson's forces killed almost everyone as we stood to protect our lands. Your grandfather Monahwee was shot seven times and still survived. And little Redbird, don't forget. It was your mother's people who sided against us at Horseshoe Bend!

My mother snatched me from my father's lap to take me to bed.

I sneaked back through the dark hallway because my mother was beginning to sing.

She wanted to be a singer before she had all of us. Before she got married. Before she worked in the fields picking cotton and green beans.

When she sang, time stopped and held me close.

REDBIRD sings as MOTHER.

SONG: A LONG TIME AGO

IT WAS A LONG TIME AGO ON THE DANCE FLOOR
YOU HELD ME IN YOUR ARMS
THE WHOLE NIGHT LONG

HA YA YA YA YA HA YA YA YA YA
HA YA YA YA YA HA YA YA YA YA

YOU TOLD ME HOW MUCH YOU LOVED ME
MORE THAN THE SUN AND THE STARS
IN THE LONG TIME AGO

I LOVE YOU, BABY, NO MATTER WHERE TIME GOES.

Light night.

After my mother sang, she and my father fought.
Their friends scattered.
I tried to pull him off her, and he went crazy.
He threw me across the room into the wall.
What happened to the storytelling father? Where did the man go who made
    my mother laugh?
He kept swinging. I got away.
I hid under the table.

REDBIRD sings.

IT WAS A LONG TIME AGO
I'LL ALWAYS LOVE YOU
IT WAS A LONG TIME AGO

SCENE 4

REDBIRD: In my family's blue-sky memory, we loved my father without ques-
    tion. We loved his laugh, his stories, his swinging us through the sky. We
    struggled with his fight, his jab, and his fear.
When I looked through my dreaming eyes, he was still a boy of four standing
    by his mother's casket. She was Monahwee's great-great-granddaughter. She
    liked to paint, blew saxophone in Indian territory and traveled about on
    Indian oil money. Still, grief from history grew in her lungs. She was dead
    of tuberculosis by her twenties. The grief had to go somewhere. We had no
    one left in our family who knew how to bury it. So it climbed onto her little
    boy's back.

REDBIRD *sings.*

JA-GAY-YOU, JAH-GAY-YOU, AHHNEE, TSA-LA-GI

SCENE 5

Light bright day.

REDBIRD: "What should I do, Little Redbird?" my mother asked me when I
was seven, as I watched her put on her makeup and uniform to get ready
for work.
"He's out with other women, chasing down their love medicine. The only time
he comes home is to eat and put on clean clothes. Don't ever fall in love,
baby."
The next Sunday morning I sat on my father's lap in the back seat of the car,
after we picked him up from jail. He smelled of old soap, whiskey, and sour
perfume; he smelled of guilt.
"What should I do, Daddy?"
"I'm sorry, baby. And tell that beautiful mother of yours I'm sorry, too."
He winked at my mother in the rearview mirror. She twisted the mirror so she
couldn't see him spy and plead.
"Sorry doesn't get it this time, Daddy. I'm over you."
I twisted in the raw pain between them. I tried to reason out the story: they
are members of enemy tribes, one came from rich and one came from poor.
One is dark; one is light. There is wrong, there is right. But there was no
way through it.

SCENE 6

Light night.

REDBIRD: One night when my father was still out late, my spirit stepped out
to look for him. At first I couldn't see anything for the fog of alcohol across
his path. I followed him to the bootlegger's, the store, and to the bar.
Then I saw him driving off alone. Come back!

Then he was gone, through the forgetting holes.

"Spirit Helper, what's the use in remembering all that? See all that dark out there? It's dangerous. It's raw stuff for black holes. They suck up everything: little girls, sad wives, men who promise you the moon and the stars."

I can't do this.

Spirit Helper reminded me, "This is your ceremony. If you stop now, you will give in to the evil."

She sang me a song, to help me make it through.

SONG: SPIRIT HELPER LULLABYE

HO-GO-SUE-GEE IS-TA-GEE, HEATH-LA-SEE, IS-TA-GEE
BEAUTIFUL BABY, BEAUTIFUL CHILD.
THE SKY IS YOUR BLANKET, THE EARTH IS YOUR CRADLE.
YOUR MOTHER ROCKS YOU CLOSE TO HER HEART.
YOUR FATHER HOLDS UP THE SKY.
HO-GO-SUE-GEE IS-TA-GEE, HEATH-LA-SEE, IS-TA-GEE

SCENE 7

REDBIRD: After our father left we didn't have time for grieving. Our mother worked more jobs.

I had to take care of the babies.

Then a flurry of suitors called on our mother.

We liked the Indian bull rider missing two fingers best.

He taught us how to loop a rope, to throw a lasso.

His heart shined with kindness whenever he walked in with hope.

And when he brought out his country guitar, we all danced silly around the kitchen table.

Marry him, we begged. Please!

No, our mother said. He's nice but what kind of job is that?

A preacher dressed in black planned to save us with a lash. He had God on his side. Get down on your knees and pray for the sins of your divorced Indian mother, your Indian father, he hissed behind her back.

We helped our mother push him and his angry God out the door.

Three times a charm, she said, when a pretty-eyed man came to call. He was
   clean. He was overly kind.
He bribed us with sweets and skates.
The yard filled up with poisonous snakes.
Watch out, we tried but couldn't tell our mother. Our tongues were stuck with
   taffy in our mouths.
We kids hid beneath the kitchen table.
And watched him unwrap our mother with a charming courting song.

Song: Flute Courting Song

He stung her with a rash of sucker darts.
Then gently wiped away her tears.
The children's room was barricaded shut from us.
It was there he kept his stacks of coins, his guns, and the piano
   he would never let us touch.
Our mother went to sleep for several years.
And that's how she was lost to us.

SCENE 8

Moonlight.

REDBIRD: When everyone else was sleeping, my spirit would leave my body
   and I'd fly free. One night I flew to the moon.
Spirit Helper met me there.
We didn't need words to talk.
Together we watched the story unwind through time and space, unraveling
   like my mother's spools of threads when I accidentally dropped them.
We saw Monahwee far away on a horse. My grandmother rode behind him
   with a baby on her back.
We saw a circle of spirit dancers around a starry fire.
A water monster whirled and whirled, punched air with its snout, then dove
   back down again.

We saw a tribal attorney leaving a meeting with oil companies. Under his arm
was a briefcase of money.
We saw my father in his truck by the lake with a case of beer.
My mother dozed on the couch at the television with the baby on her shoul-
der. The keeper yanked her by the hair and dragged her to the kitchen table.
He forced her to hold a gun loaded with one bullet, to her head. He forced
her to squeeze the trigger.
Spirit Helper talked quietly to me with her mind:
"Act carefully," she told me. "You will be tested."

SCENE 9

REDBIRD: Today he beat the baby with a belt. I can't sleep for my anger. I
want to free us. I go to the kitchen. Moonlight is full and shines a clear path
to the drawer of knives. I pick one up, me the one who is afraid to touch
knives. It's the knife our mother uses to cut chicken, to peel apples.
I stand at the door of my mother's room. She and her keeper are sleeping. Do I
pretend I am a breeze as I take his life before he sees me? Or do I wait until
the knife is at his heart, his throat, then wake him so my face is the last he
sees?
The moon flickers and I feel the answer in my gut.

SCENE 10

I have a fever. My mother prepares a pan of alcohol and water, takes off my
shirt. "I'll take over," says her keeper. My mother goes to bed. She leaves me
there.
"Lay down," he demands.
Every place he touches I turn rotten. When I am back in the room with my
brothers and sisters who are still sleeping, I pull out the killing knife and I
begin to cut away the broken.

SCENE 11

Light day.

REDBIRD: I don't remember anything after that . . . I lost the ability to fly. I disappeared.

Next thing . . . my mother and I were embracing at the bus station. Before I boarded the bus for the two-day trip to Indian school with my footlocker of everything I owned, my mother pulled out a stash of coins in a sock, that she had saved from her waitress job. And she also gave me this:

"Inside," she said, "are tobacco and a song.

There is power in this song.

But, you have to sing to wake the power up."

REDBIRD sings in response to her mother.

SONG: MOTHER'S PROTECTION SONG

YAY YAY EE YAY, YAY YAY EE YAY YAY.
YAY YAY EE YAY, YAY YAY EE YAY YAY.

I tried to give it back.

"Save yourself."

"No, baby, it doesn't work that way."

She shook her head painfully.

She walked away.

She left me there.

REDBIRD sings.

SONG: NOTHING I CAN SAY HERE

NO EARTH NO SKY
NO WINGS NO WIND
NO MOTHER NO FATHER
NO EVER AFTER OR FOREVER

NOTHING I CAN SAY
NOTHING I CAN DO
BUT WALK AWAY

BE EARTH, BE SKY
SINGS MY SPIRIT
BE WINGS, BE WIND
SINGS MY SOUL

NOTHING I CAN SAY
NOTHING I CAN DO,
I'LL BE EARTH, BE SKY
BE WINGS, BE WIND

SCENE 12

Light day.
REDBIRD drunk.

REDBIRD: I call to order the meeting of girls on restriction at Indian school.
   We broke the rules. Now we're locked up in the dorm on Saturday night.
   "Where's the dorm matron? Break out the stash. Let's dance. Give me a ticket
   for an airplane. Ain't got time to take a fast train."
We all admire Marlene; she's one of the best. She's Jackson Pollack in a dress.
   She only leaves the painting studio for sleep or work, and on Sunday she
   sneaks out to the Indian hospital on the other side of campus. She took me
   once. The children clapped and laughed when she came in. She brought
   them gifts: crayons, paper, tiny fans, all her desserts saved up for a week.
   When the staff came in, we hid. They eventually threw her out. The hospital
   carried no insurance to cover the harm she might do. Here's to you, Marlene!
And Venus Ramierez, now that's a name, and a history: one parent from the
   north on the back of a horse, the other from the south over the back of a
   river.
Venus is a singer, a real singer. Each singer has a particular gift. Some grow
   plants, some call helpers. Some heal the sick, some make the dead rise up

and dance. When Venus sings we enter into a trance. We no longer hurt
from freak chance. You're going to make it to Broadway,
Either New York, or Albuquerque!
None of us are coping well with the Bureau of Indian Affairs. We've read the
reports:
"Doesn't play well with others," "Won't speak or look us in the eyes . . . talks to
ghosts."
We hear what they are really saying: "We have the guns and money, and we
have your children."
Where's Kit? We can't find Kit anywhere.
She's not in the laundry room, practicing powwow in her underwear. She's not
out on the roof where she sneaks her smokes. She's not in the tent she made
of government-issued bedspreads, where she sketches high fashion of Indi-
ans in Paris.
Here comes Kit with a knife.
And there she goes. No top or bottom, only fury whirling in a spiritual nudity.
She's headed out into the snow.
She's what happens when someone hurts the baby.
My escape to Indian school was a success.
I present Redbird Monahwee case in point. She can corner her sheets so a
quarter spins, and knows the drill for shots, debugging, and towels. And
because she's forgotten the Indian language she learned in the cradle, she
has a chance. If we suck out her soul and put it in the closet with her ancestors' bones—she'll make it, if she doesn't blow it.

REDBIRD blows one note wildly on her sax. Sings.

WITHI-TAI-TO, GIMEE RAH
WHOA RAH NEEKO, WHOA RAH NEEKO
HEY NEY, HEY NEY, NO WAY
HEY NEY, HEY NEY, NO WAY

WITHI-TAI-TO, GIMEE RAH
WHOA RAH NEEKO, WHOA RAH NEEKO
HEY NEY, HEY NEY, NO WAY
HEY NEY, HEY NEY, NO WAY

I'M GOING BACK HOME TO CLAIM MY SOUL
TAKE IT BACK FROM THE SUGAR MAN
TAKE IT BACK FROM THE MONEY MAN
TAKE IT BACK FROM THE KEEPER MAN

WITHI-TAI-TO, GIMEE RAH
WHOA RAH NEEKO, WHOA RAH NEEKO
HEY NEY, HEY NEY, NO WAY

Sax solo, improvised.
Stomp breakdown.

SCENE 13

Light day.

REDBIRD: I went to see my mother. I saw her car in the drive. Her keeper was
supposed to be at work.
I knocked quietly first, then with sweat.
The keeper answered. "She's not here." And slammed the door.
I knocked again. I kicked the door and pounded it with my high school di-
ploma.
"Thief! I want my mom!"
Then I saw the baby at the window looking scared.
I wanted to hold her and take her out of there.
We were all trapped, even the keeper.
He could never stray far from his lair.
I turned away and found my way out of there.

SCENE 14

Party bar light.
REDBIRD dances.

REDBIRD: The first official Howling Contest took place one Saturday night out on the west mesa after the Powwow Club had closed. That night the bar didn't just close, it gave out from exhaustion. Finally, all the stuck weight of unanswered prayers, the struggle to put food on the table and buy shoes for the babies, in a city built over sacred grounds, and it all collapsed.

The howling contest was Wind's idea. She always joked: she was raised by wolves, so howling came natural. The truth was, she was raised far away from Indian country by adoptive parents who didn't know what to do when the irresistibly cute Indian baby girl grew into a troubled young woman. Wind ratted her hair out into a loose halo and she fit tight into black leather pants and jacket. She was no Pocahontas. She warmed up on forty-nine songs and Everclear. Then when she was ready she took a sip and let it rip.

A-ooooooooooooooooooooooooooooooooooooooooooooooooooo.

That tight little circle of Navajo drag queens I loved to party with was just then digging through the sand, searching for the heel of Marty's broken sateen pump. Marty always dressed the best for any occasion, and tonight in the bushes he pulled on his outfit of silk, buckskin and organdy flowers to celebrate Cher's birthday.

He was really she, except for the particulars.

Manny, Marty's companion-in-crime-against-masculinity, considered himself to be Loretta Lynn's reincarnation, even though she wasn't dead yet. Manny was the calm rudder for Marty's roller-coaster rages. Manny loved to sing. He found Marty's heel and beat out time on the car hood.

REDBIRD as MARTY sings.

I DON'T LIKE YOUR GIRLFRIEND AND HER HIGH-HEELED SHOES
WHEN YOU DANCE RIGHT PAST WITH HER IT GIVES ME THE BLUES.
YOU HAVE THE SWEETEST STEP IN DOUBLE TIME.
HOW CAN I TELL YOU THAT I LOVE YOU WHEN YOU DON'T EVEN
CARE? YOU DON'T EVEN TALK TO ME? YOU MAKE ME Sooooo—
Aooooooooooooooooooooooooooooooooooooooooooooooo—oooooo—
ooooo—ooooo

REDBIRD: "Now, finally, some competition," Wind shouted. "Okay Oklahoma girl, show us what you got there in your rooty-tooty boots. Let's hear the poetry of howl."

"C'mon!!!" yelled Marty. "You're stalling!"

The howling contest was temporarily suspended by a hulk of a man from up North, who, rumor had it, had just gotten out of prison.

He and his friends strutted up to the fire.

And as their eyes adjusted to the dark, what did they see but an Indian man in a dress.

That did it. They spit and slid up to our party with their fists.

Marty threw the first punch, with his repaired pump.

He put a nasty spin on it.

Marty's finery fooled others, but she didn't fool us. We knew she was rough.

She hit the man perfectly between the eyes, and the guy went down. Manny backed him up with a slap to one of the guy's stunned friends. This set the gnarl into a fury.

Being downed by a queen was a hundred times worse than being downed by a girl.

Everyone went wild.

Soon the whole party was punching and rolling, and those who weren't fighting were grabbing and running away with each other.

And now here came the Cavalry exactly on cue.

They flooded us with light from their circle of police cars. They had been watching in the dark all that time.

Marty was the first one dragged in and locked up. Her Cher party dress was in shreds.

I hid out behind a bush next to a man who turned out to be one of the guy-just-out-of-prison's friends.

Hey, my name's Sonny; Sonny's short for a name that's too difficult for English. And you?"

His smile sprung dimples from their nest. That's all it took.

"I'm the friend of the guy in the dress." We couldn't stop laughing at our ridiculous predicament.

After we drove over to bail out our friends, we all went for breakfast over at the all-night diner. It was packed with the pimps, prostitutes, musicians, and the rest of the hungry rough trade. Sonny turned out to be Manny's brother-in-law's cousin. We're all eventually related.

"Before we can vote on the howling contest," I announced, "I have to enter my howl." And then in that jamming restaurant, under florescent lights that made us look like we'd been up for years, I howled.

AoooooooooooooooooooooooooooooooooooooooooooooAooooooooooooooo
ooooooooooooooooAooooooooooooooooooooooooooooooooooooooooooooo
ooo.

"Okay. You win! Now stop before we get kicked out," laughed Sonny, who was
tight by my side, my friends, and the whole rest of the mess.

Dreamily.

When Sonny took my hand I just went. I didn't ask where or why or how. I
couldn't save my mother from her keeper, or keep my father from his party.
"This is my time," I said. And Time lifted up its glorious beaded head and I
latched on, and I began to fly.

SONG: THIS IS MY HEART

Sax riff.

THIS IS MY HEART. IT IS A GOOD HEART.
WEAVES A MEMBRANE OF MIST AND FIRE
WHEN WE SPEAK LOVE IN THE FLOWER WORLD
MY HEART IS CLOSE ENOUGH TO SING TO YOU IN A LANGUAGE TOO
CLUMSY FOR HUMAN WORDS.

Sax riff.

THIS IS MY HEAD. IT IS A GOOD HEAD.
IT WHIRRS, INSIDE WITH A SWARM OF WORRIES.
WHAT IS THE SOURCE OF THIS MYSTERY?
WHY CAN'T I SEE IT RIGHT HERE, RIGHT NOW AS REAL AS THESE
HANDS HAMMERING THE WORLD TOGETHER?

Sax riff.

THIS IS MY SOUL. IT IS A GOOD SOUL.
IT TELLS ME, "COME HERE FORGETFUL ONE."
AND WE SIT TOGETHER.

WE COOK A LITTLE SOMETHING TO EAT, THEN A SIP
OF SOMETHING SWEET, FOR MEMORY.

Sax solo.

SCENE 15

Light bright.

REDBIRD: As I flew with Sonny to the stars, my grandmother's stories re-
turned to me.

Light bright night.

"One night at the last stomp dance at the end of the season, when the leaves
were beginning to fall, I remember seeing him," said my grandmother.
"I was only ten. A good-looking man, from somewhere we'd never heard of
before, showed up and brightened up the place. We welcomed him, fed
him, and invited him to sit with us, to dance. It is our way to take good care
of visitors.
"Still the people are not fools. We were warned to stay within the circle. I was
awakened at dawn from my doze on the pile of quilts by the terrible cries.
Despite the precautions, we were missing one. She was the beloved daughter of the chief.
"She was wearing only a red dress and loafers. "She would never leave on her
own," my grandmother said. We never saw her again. Though the next
night, a tiny red star appeared on the horizon."

SCENE 16

Light bright day.

REDBIRD: I was happy as I made a home around the kitchen table in Sonny's
world, up here in the stars.

We had our first baby. She was beautiful like him, with a soft light from her
  dark, amber skin. Sonny loved her as my father had loved me.
I was happy except for one problem. Sonny and I quarreled. It was over his
  tree. This wasn't any ordinary tree. Sonny's tree was shimmering with deli-
  cate flowers the color somewhere between sunrise and a hickory fire flame.
  Her scent was sweeter than falling-in-love sweat. When she sang her sad
  refrain, Sonny forgot about me.
I was immediately jealous of that tree. And I had the sense she was jealous of me.
"If you touch my tree," Sonny warned me, "you will never get to go home
  again."
But his fury didn't change the way I felt about his tree.
Then I got pregnant with a son.
The birthing was hard. He pushed. My body pulled. We went back and forth
  between sky and earth. I began dying. My grandmother found me in the
  after-death realm, as I stood at the entrance to my family's encampment.
  "Go back, Redbird. It's not your time. Your babies need you." She pushed
  and after she pushed, our stolid boy found his way into the world with us.
After our son's birth, Sonny left us nights to stay with his lover, his tree. I
  couldn't sleep; I couldn't cry tears. Sonny's tree lushly bloomed, exuding her
  maddening musk. I began looking for a hole in the sky, for a way to leave.
  Tree began singing and calling out to me. I was lonely. Her voice was sweet.

REDBIRD sings as tree.

I WANT TO SEE THE CHILDREN PLAY.

REDBIRD: We became like sisters; we became friends.
One morning I was uneasy, strange.
The baby was teething and cranky as I gathered him up to take him out to the
  tree. I dressed up my daughter in her favorite dress, made with ribbons all
  the colors I was missing from earth. She danced and played as we walked
  out to the tree. Sonny's tree was sad. She was singing.

REDBIRD singing and playing flute as tree.

I FOLLOWED STARLIGHT JUST LIKE YOU,
AND THEN HE CHANGED, OR MAYBE IT WAS ME.

I WAS AN EARTH GIRL, IN A STAR WORLD
IT WASN'T WORKING, HE TURNED ME INTO A TREE.
HE'LL PLANT AND BURY YOU AS HE DID ME,
TO MAKE YOU STAY.
I'LL HELP YOU LEAVE.
PULL ME UP. BENEATH MY ROOTS YOU WILL FIND THE WAY HOME.
SAVE YOURSELF AND YOUR CHILDREN.
TO KNOW YOU'RE FREE WILL MAKE ME HAPPY.

REDBIRD: It was the hardest thing I'd ever done, but I pulled her up.
Sonny heard her cries and came running. I tucked the babies under my arms
   and stood at the edge where her roots now dangled. He grabbed us and I
   tried to pull free. It was then I heard my mother's voice at the bus station.
   "Sing to wake up the power! Sing!"

REDBIRD sings.

SONG: MOTHER'S PROTECTION SONG

YAY YAY EE YAY, YAY YAY EE YAY YAY.
YAY YAY EE YAY, YAY YAY EE YAY YAY.

REDBIRD: My mother's song flew out and wrapped us in its arms. Sonny
   slipped his grasp and we fell free. We fell and fell and fell, flying through the
   hole in the sky. We flew through time like Monahwee on his black horse.
   My two babies were soon grown. They branched out on their own. And
   though we made it through difficult years, something was wrong.
I was still falling.

SONG: FALLING, FALLING

ONE PART OF ME SPEAKS THE SACRED LANGUAGE OF FIRE.
THE OTHER PART UNDERSTANDS IN BROKEN HEART.

MY MIND CAN'T MAKE UP ITS CRAZY MIND,
WHEN I'M BURDENED BY RAINCLOUDS OF DESIRE.

FALLING, FALLING.
FALLING, FALLING.

I DIDN'T WANT TO MAKE THE SAME MISTAKES,
I HAD TO FIND MY OWN BRIGHT STAR.

TOUCH MY SKIN AND I WANT BACK IN AGAIN.
DON'T LEAVE ME HERE INSIDE, ALONE.

FALLING, FALLING.
FALLING, FALLING.

I LOST EVERYTHING FOR LOVE.
I HAD NO PLACE ELSE TO GO, BUT HOME.

SCENE 17

Light bright day.

REDBIRD: I went to find my mother. I went to her door. No one answered.
The keeper still had his hold. The danger with evil is it becomes habit.
"What can I do?" I asked Spirit Helper.
She answered, "If you can't talk to your mother in person, you can talk to her
spirit."
I invited my mother's spirit to come and speak with me.
Then before I knew it, there sat the spirit of my mother, my mother! My
mother!
She smelled of tenderness. She smelled of love without question. I wanted this
feeling, forever.
My mother's spirit moved to go.
"But why?" I asked her.
"Why can't I come home?"

"Why?" I begged without a rag of pride, "Did you keep him
and not me when I told you what happened?"
"You need to know this," her spirit said.
"I dreamed a daughter who wanted to be born. I had been up writing songs
   all night at the kitchen table, when you appeared to me. I saw you first as
   a baby with fat cheeks, and then there you were, a grown woman, just like
   you are now. And I asked you then, 'Why come into this kind of world?
   This is not a good time.'
But your intent made a fine unwavering line that connected your heart to
   mine."
My mother's spirit stood up to leave. I called after her:
"You're going back to him! Do you love him more than me, more than all of
   us?"
Then she was gone.
Spirit Helper said, "There are some things that take an eternity to understand."
Then Spirit Helper sang a healing song.

SONG: SHINING PERSONS ARRIVE

HERE HEALING SONG

SHINING PERSONS ARRIVE HERE
HYVTKE LANI
OPEN YOUR BEING
HYVTKE JADE
WITH EVERY SMALL THOUGHT OF WHAT TO FIX
WITH EVERY IMMENSE THOUGHT OF DANCERS WINDING
THROUGH THE MILKY WAY
HYVTKE LVSTE
WHAT OBSCURES, FALLS AWAY
HYVTKE HVTKE

SCENE 18

Midnight.
The father's body is in state.

REDBIRD: I followed your tracks and finally found you, Daddy.
I wrapped your body in your favorite ceremonial blanket.
I used to follow you everywhere.
Remember that time you brought home a deer?
I followed you as you unloaded it from the truck. I helped as you strung the
  deer up in the tree. I squatted down with you as the red sun kissed the red
  earth. You tamped out some tobacco into our hands. You said, "We pray
  with tobacco to acknowledge the spirit of the deer. We give thanks, Mvto,
  mvto.
There is much suffering on this earth. Even plants suffer. Tobacco is a medi-
  cine, a gift from the Creator."
And remember I said: "But Daddy, you smoke three packs of Lucky Strikes a
  day!"
I was such a little plant, drinking in your words. "And what about whiskey,
  Dad?" I asked you.
"I'm sorry, Hokte. It's killing me," you said. "Pray for me, girl."
Time turned its back on you and me, Daddy.

REDBIRD places some tobacco on her father's blanket.
Devastated.

This is for you, for your journey. Go! Find the way home. Pray for me.

SCENE 19

After light night.
REDBIRD is driving drunk.

REDBIRD: I feel crazy, like Grandfather Monahwee in the middle of the
  slaughter.
I never was a warrior for justice; I left my brothers and sisters . . . Where are

Kit and Venus from Indian school? Marty or Manny was shot in front of a
gay bar just for being himself.
"I can't leave him now," said my mother about the keeper. Why didn't my father come back and save all of us?
I'm getting out of here. I'll find my daughter. We'll take my son to rehab. Let's
see what this horse can do.

Squealing tires. Car crash: terrible clatter of flying metal.
Blackout.

SCENE 20

Light; GUARDIAN MUSICIAN in shadow.
Voice-over in REDBIRD's voice.

I curled up in the dark with a terrible silence in my heart. Then I heard my
grandmother singing.

REDBIRD as grandmother sings a refrain from the Trail of Tears song.

REDBIRD: And I felt myself lifted up.
"Once the world was perfect, Granddaughter, and we were happy in that
world. Then we took it for granted. Discontent began a small rumble in the
earthly mind.
Then Doubt pushed through with its spiked head, and all manner of demon
thoughts jumped through.
We destroyed the world we had been given. Each stone of jealousy, each stone
of fear, greed, and envy put out the light.
No one was without a stone in his or her hand.
There we were, right back where we had started.
We were bumping into each other in the dark.
Then, one of the stumbling ones took pity on another and shared their
blanket.
A spark of kindness made a light."

REDBIRD appears onstage carrying a basket of food and goods.

REDBIRD: Spirit Helper brought me home again to this table. Everything you need for your healing is here, she told me.

"The table is within you; it has always been within you. You must remember to acknowledge the gifts. You must remember to share," she said. Then she gave me her shawl.

This giveaway is in honor of our ceremony tonight, in honor of all the gifts of struggle of every one of us here.

Gifts are shared with the audience in this traditional giveaway.

CLOSING

SONG: GOIN' HOME

LAST DANCE AND THE NIGHT IS ALMOST OVER.
ONE LAST ROUND UNDER THE STARRY SKY.

WE'RE ALL GOING HOME SOMEWAY, SOMEHOW WHEN IT'S OVER.

HEY E YAH, HEY E YAY, AYE E YAH AYE E YAY

Sax riff.

IF YOU'VE FOUND LOVE IN THE CIRCLE, THEN HOLD ONTO IT,
NOT TOO TIGHT.
IF YOU HAVE TO LET LOVE GO, THEN LET IT GO. KEEP ON DANCING.

I DON'T CARE IF YOU'RE MARRIED SIXTEEN TIMES
I'LL GET YOU YET.

GOIN' HOME GOIN' HOME

Sax solo leading into silence.

I'M FROM OKLAHOMA GOT NO ONE TO CALL MINE

A LOVE SUPREME, A LOVE SUPREME
A LOVE SUPREME, A LOVE SUPREME

In the break.

EVERYBODY WANTS THAT SWEET SWEET LOVE SUPREME

Sax riff.

WHEN THE DANCE IS OVER, SWEETHEART, TAKE ME HOME
IN YOUR ONE-EYED FORD.
(Speaks) BUT WE GOTTA STOP AND PICK UP GRANDMA,
ALL OF MY AUNTS, MY CHILDREN . . .

GOIN' HOME GOIN' HOME

IT'S TIME TO GO HOME NOW. BE KIND TO ALL YOU MEET
ALONG THE WAY. MYTO MVTO. HOLD ONTO SOMEBODY'S HAND
THROUGH THE DARK.

KUL-KU-CE CV-NA-KĒ, HV-YA-YI-CA-RES,
KUL-KU-CE CV-NA-KĒ, HV-YA-YI-CA-RES,
KUL-KU-CE CV-NA-KĒ, HV-YA-YI-CA-RES,
KUL-KE-KVS, KUL-KE-KVS, KUL-KE-KVS

END OF PLAY

Reflections on Joy Harjo, Indigenous Feminism, and Experiments in Creative Expression

I want to tell you when I think of culture, I think of rupture, something split open trying to put itself back together again.

I know something was taken away from me. I know that what I have, I had to beg, borrow, and steal it away in small snatches for it to be mine.

As a child, I sat in the corner of the kitchen hoping that none of the aunties would think I was in the way. Or worse, that their topic of conversation wasn't meant for my ears and I would be banished, sent to play with my dolls or find something to watch on TV.

I want to tell you that a very different kind of pain settles in around so much silence and solitude.

I remember my mother, sitting, drinking wine, and laughing. One of the cousins asks, "But what are we?"

She'd shrug her shoulders and laugh. Her reply, as she shook her head decidedly from left to right: "We're Mexican (head to the left). We're Indian (head to the right)."

She'd laugh some more. "We're Mexican. We're Indian."

And then we'd sit there even more confused than before we had piped up with the question.

"What are we?"

My mother's mother was Lila, and she was Wiyot. She was born and raised on a reservation until she met and married my grandfather, Raymond. Lila's tribe is from the far northern coastal section of California. Raymond's family was from the geographic area now known as Arizona in the Southwest region of the United States. Once upon a time it was Mexico.

I can still hear her laughter, "We're Mexican. We're Indian."

We're Mexican but we don't speak Spanish. We're Indian but we don't know what that means. And our last name is Page.

My mother refused to speak Spanish in our bicultural home. Spanish from her mouth as a child meant that she would be beaten by her teachers in the

Oakland Public Schools. Back in the day, the teachers walked around with rulers and hit your hands if you spoke Spanish in their classrooms. She, like so many mothers, wanted to protect her children. She wanted to spare us the suffering that she knew all too well.

My mother despised the kitchen in our home and everything about cooking. As a young wife and stay-at-home mom, she learned to prepare dinners the way my Anglo father preferred them. We ate family meals together while she complained about how much she hated to cook. As I got older, I became her quiet confidante. I don't remember when I was invited for the first time to join her in the kitchen, but I know another world opened up to me. I was invited to the table that my mother and her sisters shared. I learned that there were things that she loved to cook and, more important, that she loved to eat. She and my aunts came together around food, and the meals they shared were very different from the steak, potatoes, and canned vegetables that constituted most of our family dinners. Refried beans had to soak overnight before you could start cooking them. Handmade tortillas that Rose and Delores took so much care and time to make were perfectly round and flat. We ate them hot off the grill, slathered with melting butter. Linda used ancho chilis and other savory spices to make enchiladas. She warned us not to touch our eyes or nose after handling these peppers. One of my mother's favorites was spicy chorizo with eggs that were fried to perfection together in one pan and eaten with tortillas. Another favorite of hers were tacos. We used the freshest ingredients: tomatoes, green onions, cheese, lettuce, avocado, grilled meat, beans with Spanish rice on the side. We fried corn tortillas into crisp shells that each woman filled to her own liking.

As a young adult, I would visit my mother and she would ask, "Why don't you make some chorizo and eggs?" or "What do you think of making tacos for us for dinner?" A special invitation for her daughter. And with the meals came the stories and the gossip and the fights. The laughter and the tears.

It wasn't until her passing in 2005 that I realized my special status with her, with my aunts, and our relationship to food. My brother had no idea that my mother would eat chorizo and eggs with tortillas for breakfast. It wasn't until he and I had a disagreement about what she ate that I realized he was never at our special meals. Neither he nor my father sat at our table. This food, this key element to my identity, was passed from mother to daughter. Food does more than satisfy hunger. It deepens our understanding of who we are, and it brings us closer to one another when we share it. Our family, our lives, our culture is produced at our kitchen tables. It took me a long time to learn this lesson, and it all hit home the first time I read Joy Harjo's "Perhaps the World Ends Here" in *The Woman Who Fell from the Sky* (W. W. Norton, 1994).

I was a young mother and college student in Hayward, California. I had little in common with my peers. And then, in a women's studies course, I encountered Joy's work and I felt a seismic shift. I wasn't alone, and I wasn't as crazy as I had started to feel at that large state institution in my hometown.

The bittersweet poem captures all of the elements of life, and links our livelihood to the kitchen table where we take in food in order to live. I learned my most valuable lessons at my mother's table. If the world might end there, that's because it definitely began there: "We have given birth on this table, and have prepared our parents for burial here"; the kitchen table is the place where "we sing with joy, with sorrow. We pray of suffering and remorse. We give thanks" (Harjo 1994, 6). These things and more came to pass at my mother's table.

I had no idea, when I first read this poem in the late 1990s, that I would meet Joy Harjo a decade later in Westfield, Massachusetts. At that time, I was living and working in the nearby town of Amherst after completing my MFA in theater at the University of Massachusetts–Amherst. Magdalena Gomez, an extraordinary poet and dear friend, told me about Joy's reading and I decided to go. I had recently lost an aunt, my mother's youngest sister Linda, and did not have enough money to travel home for her funeral. On a cold, wintry night, I sat alone in the crowded auditorium and wept while Joy read her poems and played her saxophone.

I had been reading and studying her poetry for a long time and felt a gravitational pull toward her that I couldn't quite name. I wasn't simply a fan of her work; rather, I felt that she was writing about my life and the women in my family. Her poetry is powerful, yes. But that night, I wept because I saw Aunt Linda in her. The two women look strikingly similar. So much so that they could have been sisters. I wept for the many losses that Linda endured in her life. I kept thinking that if my mother and her sisters and their mother had found their voices and been listened to, like Joy, then maybe their lives would have turned out differently. I wept because I didn't know how to help them.

When the reading ended and the room cleared out, I moved closer to the stage. Joy was graciously speaking to a few women who had made their way to her. I didn't plan to speak to her, and I didn't know exactly why I had moved so close to her, but within a few minutes, she was sitting in front of me. I thanked her for her powerful poetry and then told her how much she favored my aunt Linda. The tears started up again. She took my hand and said, "Tell me about your aunt."

I don't recall my exact words, but I do know that I told her about my aunt's difficult life wrought with physical abuse, drug addiction, poverty, and loss. Then I told Joy how connected I felt to her poem "Remember" (Harjo 1983). In its opening line, she offers this directive: "Remember the sky that you were born under, know each of the stars' stories." My sense of spiritualty aligns with Joy's command to honor the higher powers of the natural world and to acknowledge my place in the universe. In the second line, her tone shifts as she continues: "Remember the moon, know who she is. I met her in a bar once in Iowa City" (35). Grounded in an urban reality, I often find it difficult to recognize spirit in places like bars. But Joy's poem reminds me that the moon, with her grace and compassion, is just as likely to show up in a bar as anyplace else. (In subsequent publications, Harjo has edited this line out of the poem.) Then, I told her about the alcoholism in my family and its toll on all of us. She asked me about my people, and I explained to her that my ancestors were Wiyot but that none of the elders in my family would talk to the younger generations about this.

Joy responded by telling me that she had visited the story of the Wiyot people many times and actually went to the reservation once. She told me that my people endured horrific violence and attempts at genocide. When white settlers arrived in the geographic region now known as California, they tried to wipe out the entire population of Wiyots. Those who survived went into hiding to preserve their lives. She explained that this tragedy, like so many for Native Americans, has gone unspoken for a very long time. I was stunned by this information, and we sat and held hands for a few minutes more.

This seemingly small gesture—Joy sitting, listening, and holding my hand—meant a great deal to me. Over the next decade, we stayed in touch and developed a friendship. Her poetry and my conversations with her inspired me to tell my story and to honor my ancestors through my writing. I have done more research on my people and the legacy of trauma they experienced. I now know more about the pain, the silence, and the power of speaking out and speaking truth to power even if our numbers are small, even in the face of genocide. Joy helped me tremendously in my journey with her generosity that evening. She is a prolific writer and a tireless performer who won the 2015 Wallace Stevens Award recognizing her outstanding mastery of poetry (Alicia Ostriker, Academy of American Poets). Her writing continues to inspire me and, I am sure, many others.

———

Wings of Night Sky, Wings of Morning Light, her most recent performative endeavor, blends poetry, music, and theater. Harjo presented a workshop production of this play at the Native Theater Festival at the Public Theater in New York in 2007. In 2009, Randy Reinholz, theater director and University of California San Diego professor, directed the play at Native Voices at the Autry, where he is one of the founding co-producers. In the promotional materials, Reinholz describes the play as "a heightened ceremony, a broad intersection of art forms, an intimate act that celebrates the beauty and the inherent paradoxes of the human condition" (Native Voices press release, March 2009).

I attended the workshop production of an early version of the piece at the Public Theater and the panel discussion that immediately followed it in December 2007. There was a mixed reaction from the audience members during the talk, and I remember thinking that Harjo was very brave to show new work and then endure immediate responses from panelists and audience members. As a dramaturg who has organized post-show discussions for new plays, I can relate to the challenges of balancing respect for the artist and her process with creating a space for audiences to respond to the work they have just seen. I think a facilitator's primary role in this type of conversation is to provide context for the audience members while striving to elicit useful and meaningful feedback for the artists. Sadly, the facilitator for this particular conversation fell short. To be fair, post-show discussions are difficult to manage, and there is usually a very limited amount of time during which one can both frame a conversation and move it in a productive way for the artist, in this case Harjo. With a dramaturgical framework that connects Harjo's poetry, music, and performance text, in this essay I will highlight major themes in the work that connect to larger ideas about indigenous feminism and experimental performance practice. This kind of care and attention must be paid to Native American theater, its history, its cultural specificity, its forms, and its purpose, if theater practitioners and producers truly want to support ongoing work by Native American playwrights.

Harjo's blend of poetry and music to tell the story of Redbird, the central character in *Wings of Night Sky, Wings of Morning Light*, signals Harjo's departure from conventional notions of storytelling. In order to create this performance text, she incorporated concepts and imagery from her 1994 poem "Perhaps the World Ends Here" and music from her two latest CDs: *Winding through the Milky Way* (2008) and *Red Dreams: A Trail Beyond Tears* (2010). Taken together, these three works demonstrate Harjo's long-standing focus on articulating her place in the cosmos, a location that is rooted in contemporary urban reality as much as the realm of the ancestors and spirit guides.

In *Wings of Night Sky, Wings of Morning Light*, Harjo sets the scene with a description of the kitchen table, placed just left of center stage. The kitchen table is "[t]he gut around which all action flows. It is a heart, a bed, a bier, a car, a counter at the bar, an altar, and a hiding place" (2007, 19). This stage direction signals from the very beginning that this play is not grounded in realism: instead, metaphor and magic abound. The table is all things and figures prominently in all of the action of the performance. This is a literal translation of the significance of the kitchen table in "Perhaps the World Ends Here," where Harjo writes the opening line "The world begins at a kitchen table. No matter what we must eat to live." By the end of the poem, she ponders, "Perhaps the world will end at the kitchen table, while we are laughing and crying, eating of the last sweet, bite" (1994, 68) In this poem, Harjo takes the reader on a journey through life. Fifteen years later, she mirrors the structure of this poem in Redbird's cosmic journey in *Wings of Night Sky, Wings of Morning Light*. In both the 1994 poem and the 2007 performance text, the reader is keenly aware of the cyclical movement through life. Redbird's journey begins in crisis as we are asked by Redbird's relative to "[p]lease keep in mind that the patient Redbird Monahwee is in a delicate and vulnerable state. There is imbalance between dark and light. We need your good thoughts to help see us through." The unnamed relative then introduces the audience to Redbird's protector guardian, who "open[s] with a traditional family story and song, so that our minds come together as one" (2007, 3). The blurring of the roles of Relative, Spirit Helper, and Redbird, all played by Harjo (in the full production at Native Voices at the Autry) facilitates the audience's understanding of the close relationship between each of the characters. As Harjo embodies each of the characters, she moves seamlessly from one to the other onstage.

Redbird's life unfolds before us, and we witness the roots of her distress that date back before her birth. In Scene 2, Harjo writes:

When my spirit crossed worlds to join my father and mother, there were no songs to assist the birth.
There was no cedar or tobacco . . . but—my mother had drugs!
My body was a wet, ripe, bloody seed
And it was about to be spit onto concrete in Oklahoma.
That's when I changed my mind. (2007, 8)

In this short description, we learn that Redbird's parents no longer had access to the traditional songs or medicinal herbs to assist in her birth, and that they lived in a city. Just before her birth, Redbird understands that she will be "spit onto the red earth of Oklahoma" (8). This harsh image signals the enduring strife of urban reality that many indigenous people face in the United States. Her guardian convinces her to proceed with her birth, and the play is set in motion.

Harjo also works with the journey motif in her 2008 CD *Winding through the Milky Way*. "Rabbit Is Up to Tricks" is the first song for both *Wings of Night Sky, Wings of Morning Light* and *Winding through the Milky Way*. With this song, listeners embark on a journey that begins "a long time ago." Harjo sings, "In a world long before this one, there was enough for everyone until somebody got out of line." Through the CD, we experience a journey of the soul. In "This Is My Heart," the second track, Harjo declares, "This is my soul. It is a good soul. It tells me, 'Come here forgetful one.' We sit together. We cook a little something to eat. Then a sip of something sweet. For memory." Near the end of the CD, in "Witchi Tai To," Harjo tells us, "I went back home to claim my soul/took it back/ from the sugarman/took it back from the money man/took it back from the devil man." We have moved with her from a time of forgetfulness and confusion to a time of self-determination. Embedded in this personal journey is a critique of colonialism. Harjo claims power and sovereignty over herself in the way that indigenous people (and people of color in the United States) struggle to be free from oppression in its many forms. Freedom, in the context of *Winding through the Milky Way*, is found at the end of the metaphoric night in the song "Goin' Home." She sings, "We're all goin' home some way, some how," and finally she instructs, "Be kind to all you meet along the way. We're all related in this place" (Harjo 2008).

Redbird, the protagonist in *Wings of Night Sky, Wings of Morning Light*, takes this same journey across time and place in order to become fully actualized. Harjo describes Redbird as "a native woman, Mvskoke, somewhere in her later twenties, thirties, forties, or fifties" (2007, 2), making Redbird an everywoman of sorts and drawing on an allegorical approach to storytelling. This reinforces the idea of our connectedness to each other across time and space that Harjo establishes at the beginning of the play with her decision to portray all of the characters.

Harjo places the song "Rabbit Is Up to Tricks" at the beginning of her play, and this cautionary tale forewarns of unchecked selfishness and greed: "In a world long before this one, there was enough for everyone until somebody got out of line" (2007, 4). That someone is Rabbit, who was bored; clay man is Rabbit's

Joy Harjo and Larry Mitchell. Production still from *Wings of Night Sky,
Wings of Morning Light*, March 2009. Photo by Silvia Mautner.

Joy Harjo, "It was at this kitchen table I was forbidden to sing when I was fourteen."
Production still from *Wings of Night Sky, Wings of Morning Light,*
March 2009. Photo by Silvia Mautner.

Joy Harjo, "I hid under the table." Production still from
Wings of Night Sky, Wings of Morning Light, March 2009. Photo by Silvia Mautner.

Joy Harjo, "We saw Monahwee far away on a horse."
Production still from *Wings of Night Sky, Wings of Morning
Light*, March 2009. Photo by Silvia Mautner.

Joy Harjo (with Larry Mitchell): "I present Redbird Monahwee."
Production still from *Wings of Night Sky, Wings of Morning Light,*
March 2009. Photo by Silvia Mautner.

Joy Harjo and Larry Mitchell at the end of the play. Production still from *Wings of Night Sky, Wings of Morning Light*, March 2009. Photo by Silvia Mautner.

Institute of American Indian Arts Art Department Faculty, circa 1966:
Ralph Pardington (*back row*); Leo Bushman, James McGrath, Louis Ballard
(*second row from top, left to right*); Seymour Tubis, Neil Parsons, Rolland Meinholtz,
Lloyd New, Kay Weist, Terry Allen, Allan Houser, Fritz Scholder, Michael McCormick
(*middle row, left to righ*t); Otellie Loloma, Terence Shubert, Josephine Wapp
(*front row, left to right*). Photo courtesy of IAIA Archives, Santa Fe, NM.

Rolland Meinholtz, Joy Harjo, William S. Yellow Robe, Jr. (*left to right*).
Photo taken at the Public Theater, 2007.

From *Deep Roots, Tall Cedar*, Institute of American Indian Arts, theater performance 1, 1968: Joy Harjo and Jane Lind (*left, behind screen*); Keith Conway (*kneeling in front*); Phillip Wilmon (*right, behind screen*). Photo Courtesy of the U.S. Department of the Interior, Indian Arts and Crafts Board.

From *Deep Roots, Tall Cedar*, Institute of American Indian Arts, theater performance 2, 1968. *Far left, seated*: Phillip Wilmon; *center, back, seated*: Tom Adams; *right, standing*: Keith Conway; *far right, seated*: Cordell Morsette. Photo Courtesy of the U.S. Department of the Interior, Indian Arts and Crafts Board.

creation. Rabbit entertains himself by teaching clay man to steal things, cultivating greed and selfishness in this newly formed companion. Harjo describes clay man as insatiable, a man who wanted "all the wives," "all the gold." She leaps from one greedy man and implicates us all when she writes, "Soon it was countries, and then it was trade. The wanting infected the earth." Clay man's greed is our greed, the very greed that drives our capitalist society. Linking back to a sense of community, Harjo writes that we have been conditioned to "forget our songs, our stories." She concludes, "We could no longer see or hear our ancestors, or talk with each other across the kitchen table" (2007, 5).

We quickly move to the present time and learn that Redbird feels lost and angry. We learn that her stepfather, whom she calls "the keeper," has forbidden her to sing in her home. She sits with Spirit Helper at the kitchen table, where she is instructed to go back to the beginning of her story: the time of her birth and the struggles she and her mother had in that process. Redbird didn't want to be "spit onto the red earth of Oklahoma" where "there were no songs to assist the birth" (2007, 8). Her people were already lost before her birth, so it stands to reason that she would be lost, too. Redbird was born to two broken parents. Her trauma begins before her birth. It follows her through her young adult life; it moves with her from the domestic sphere into the colonial space of the Indian boarding school, and then into the bar where she meets her future husband Sonny. In fact, the legacy of the trauma of imperialism reaches across multiple generations and carries violent events through time. In Scene 14, Redbird finds her voice and sets out on her own path, free from home and school. She says, "This is my time. And, Time lifted up its glorious beaded head and I latched on, and I began to fly" (23).

The plot takes another turn as Redbird creates her own domestic space. Scene 16 begins in a "light bright day" with Redbird's declaration, "I was happy as I made a home around the kitchen table in Sonny's world, up here in the stars" (2007, 24). She describes the world as Sonny's, so the reader/audience is not totally surprised when things take a turn for the worse for Redbird in his domain. In highly metaphoric language, Harjo depicts a bond between the women who free themselves from Sonny. She writes this woman, who is Sonny's lover, as a tree who is saddened to be bound by her roots. Redbird, at first jealous of the tree and resentful of Sonny's affections toward the tree, becomes attracted to her songs. Redbird says, "I was lonely. Her voice was sweet" (25). The two women are able to leave when Redbird pulls the tree out by her roots. It is the women's bond to each other that allows them to literally seize their freedom together.

This action sends Redbird singing into a free fall where she meets the soul of her living mother in the spirit realm, and where she makes peace with the death of her father. While Redbird's relationship with her mother remains unreconciled, Spirit Helper guides her to her grandmother. The Creek prayer/song that was a part of the invocation at the beginning of the play returns as a reprise and serves to bind Redbird to her grandmother: "Do not get tired. Don't be discouraged. Be determined, to all come in. We will go to the highest place. We will go together" (2007, 30).

And then, we move full circle. The play opened with a call for prayers for Redbird, who was in "a delicate and vulnerable state" (2007, 3). It closes with Spirit Helper telling Redbird that she has all she needs for healing. It is all at her kitchen table, and the table is within her. Like the CD *Winding through the Milky Way*, *Wings of Night Sky, Wings of Morning Light* ends with the song "Goin' Home." Redbird's journey toward healing leads her home with a sense of responsibility to share with others in a traditional giveaway. Redbird's individual wellness is directly connected to the wellness and well-being of her family and her community. The principle of social responsibility is embedded in the cultural practice of the giveaway, where one acknowledges the blessing of his or her bounty by sharing it with others. In the play, Redbird's gift is her voice, and once she secures it, she is able to give back to her loved ones. This play also functions as a giveaway, as Harjo's bountiful gift is her storytelling, and she shares her bounty willingly and generously with the reader/audience. Shelley Scott writes that through "witnessing their performances, embodied healing can be shared by the audience and wider community" (Wilmer, 135). Redbird's strength and stability become models for the readers or audience members who face similar struggles.

———

Shari Huhndorf, professor of ethnic studies and Native American studies at the University of California–Berkeley, published *Mapping the Americas: The Transnational Politics of Contemporary Native Culture* in 2009. This book offers a pointed critique of cultural nationalism, asserts a lens of indigenous feminism through which we can study culture and politics, and demonstrates the transnational nature of indigenous peoples. In her coda titled "Border Crossings," Huhndorf examines Shelley Niro's artwork, specifically the 1997 mixed-media installation *The Border*, to drive home her central argument that "the tribal and the transnational are inseparable" and that this concept "foregrounds new critical questions" regarding "Native cultural practices" (177).

Huhndorf expertly describes contemporary Native theater and performance as the site where artists depict the urban locale as "a key center of indigenous experience." She notes that the "return to tribal communities is a major theme in the Native literary renaissance period" (114) and that "movements from tribal home to urban center find a place, however neglected, in Native literary production, including theater" (115). She also notes that this is "not yet a sustained area of literary scholarship" (115). While there is a rich and growing body of literary work worthy of study, few scholars have taken up the task of thinking and writing about it. *Native Traces: Indigenous North American Drama: A Multivocal History*, edited by Birgit Däwes, and *Native American Performance and Representation*, edited by S. E. Wilmer, are two recent books that focus on contemporary Native American performance and provide important historical context and analysis, while Christy Stanlake's 2009 book *Native American Drama: A Critical Perspective* provides dramaturgical insights, paying special attention to nine contemporary Native American plays. Lastly, editors Ann Elizabeth Armstrong, Kelli Lyon Johnson, and William A. Wortman published *Performing Worlds into Being*, using performances and papers presented at "Honoring Spiderwoman Theater/Celebrating Native American Theater," convened by the Native American Women Playwrights Archive and Miami University (Ohio) in February 2007. This book rightfully places Spiderwoman Theater as a beacon of innovation in Native American theater. Scholars Ann Haugo, associate professor of theater at Illinois State University, and Jaye T. Darby, co-founder and co-director with Hanay Geiogamah of Project HOOP (Honoring Our Origins and People through Native Theater) at UCLA, have each written important essays that outline the details of the Native American cultural renaissance of the 1960s and 1970s. There is an ongoing need for the documentation and analysis of contemporary Native American theater.

Haugo, in her chapter titled "Native American Drama: A Historical Survey" in *Native Traces*, provides a comprehensive survey of Native theater and marks the beginning of the contemporary Native theater movement with the founding of three important companies: Native American Theater Ensemble by Hanay Geiogamah in 1972 at La MaMa Experimental Theater in New York; Red Earth Performing Arts in Seattle in 1974; and Spiderwoman Theater, composed of Gloria Miguel, Muriel Miguel, and Lisa Mayo in 1975, also in New York. In Haugo's chronicle, the arc of contemporary Native cultural production has its roots in the literary boom of the late 1960s. She notes that this can be marked by the publication of the novel *The House Made of Dawn* by N. Scott Momaday in 1968, winner of the Pulitzer Prize for literature. Additional significant works of that time include *Custer Died for Your Sins* by Vine Deloria Jr. in 1969, James Welch's *Winter in the Blood* in 1974, the poetry collections *Going for the Rain* in 1976 and *A Good Journey* in 1977 by Simon Ortiz, and *Ceremony* by Leslie Marmon Silko in 1979. It was at this time that Harjo began writing poetry in response to the Native Rights organizing and the creative expression that was blossoming. This decade, according to Haugo, "marks a moment when Native theater artists began to have a greater degree of control over their own work by running companies, writing plays and directing productions" (43).

Of equal importance, this time period also saw the rise of the American Indian Movement across the United States. Jaye T. Darby begins her chapter "People with Strong Hearts: Staging Communitism in Hanay Geiogamah's Plays *Body Indian* and *49*" in *Native American Performance and Representation* with a succinct description of the inciting incidents of the Red Power movement. The artists, activists, and intellectuals of this movement did not separate their livelihood, their art, their culture, or their politics into distinct categories, much like the well-documented sisterhood of the Black Power and Black Arts movements; the relationships between organizers of the Brown Power movement, the United Farm Workers and Teatro Campesino; and the Young Lords political organizing efforts and the Nuyorican Arts movement. Darby writes that the goals of the Red Power movement were "sovereignty and cultural autonomy" (164). In her analysis of *Body Indian* and *49*, Darby illustrates the presence of these goals in each of the protagonists' journeys. The same can be said of Harjo's *Wings of Night Sky, Wings of Morning Light* and her character Redbird's path to healing and wholeness. Redbird's recovery exemplifies what bell hooks calls the "love ethic" that is necessary in the struggle for liberation. In her essay "Love as a Practice of Freedom," hooks writes that it is by "beginning with love as the ethical foundation for politics, that we are best positioned to transform society in ways that enhance the collective good" (247).

Harjo's performance text *Wings of Night Sky, Wings of Morning Light* is also an assertion of indigenous feminism that specifically explores issues of gender and sexuality. With this text, Harjo joins the theatrical continuum that Shari Huhndorf establishes in her chapter titled "Indigenous Feminism, Performance and Memory" (2009, 105–39). Huhndorf's book includes the early and ongoing work of Spiderwoman Theater alongside plays by Monica Mojica and Marie Clements. Again, Ann Haugo has completed in-depth work with her chapter "'Circles upon Circles upon Circles': Native Women in Theater and Performance," published in Geiogamah and Darby's *American Indian Theater in Performance: A Reader*. Taken together, the performance texts of these women articulate concepts of indigenous women that address questions of sovereignty as intertwined with gender equity. In *Indigenous Women and Feminism: Politics, Activism, and Culture*, Huhndorf and Cheryl Suzack describe expressions of indigenous feminism and cite human rights activist Elsie B. Redbird, who says, "If the erosion of sovereignty comes from disempowering women, its renewed strength will come from re-empowering them" (6).

Harjo depicts a chaotic world for Redbird to navigate. On her journey, her early encounters with her father are bittersweet, and then he leaves the family. Redbird recounts stories of her "great-great-grandfather," who was the best horse trader and who knew how to bend time (2007, 9). These stories move quickly from nostalgia to trauma as her father states, "The only race I have is outrunning the Whiteman" (9). He asks for another beer, and later in the scene, things take a violent turn. Harjo writes, "He kept swinging. I got away. I hid under the table" (11). The men in her life, namely the keeper (the man who replaces her father in her mother's home) and Redbird's first husband, continue to perpetuate violence throughout the play. Using Huhndorf's analysis, these men colonize the domestic space of the home. This oppression on an intimate level mirrors the larger systemic violence enacted on Native American people. In fact, throughout the play, Redbird moves from one colonial space to another as she moves from her childhood home to the Indian boarding school and then to her home "in the stars" with Sonny, where they start a family (24). None of these colonized domestic spaces suffice, and Redbird remains unsettled until she recognizes that her sense of freedom must come from within. Redbird's journey is one toward self-determination on an individual level, a spiritual level, and a communal level.

Harjo connects Redbird's journey toward freedom to her sexuality. In Scene 10, Redbird experiences sexual trauma at the hands of the keeper. At the beginning of Scene 11, Redbird states, "I don't remember anything after that . . . I lost the ability to fly. I disappeared" (2007, 16). The scene then abruptly jumps to Redbird's departure to boarding school. While violence and sexual aggression are enacted by some of the men in this play, it is a misreading to blame all of the men for Redbird's struggles. On a visit home from boarding school, Redbird attempts to see her mother, and the keeper prevents her from doing so. With a mixture of anger and agonizing compassion, Redbird states plainly, "We were all trapped, even the keeper" (20). Again, the larger context of imperial violence permeates the home and poisons intimate relationships. The public and the private realm are more connected than not.

While Harjo is linked to the tradition of indigenous feminist women artists such as Gloria Miguel, Muriel Miguel, and Lisa Mayo of Spiderwoman Theater, as well as Monica Mojica, Victoria Nalani Knuebuhl, and Cherríe Moraga, she is also linked aesthetically to a community of artists who work with jazz aesthetics and performance. Omi Osun Joni L. Jones has documented this type of work as it was practiced in the Austin Project at the University of Texas–Austin from 2002 to 2007. The resulting book, *Experiments in a Jazz Aesthetic: Art, Activism, Academia, and the Austin Project*, is a useful pedagogical tool and an archive of creative writing and reflection by workshop leaders and participants. Osun describes the jazz aesthetic as being forged from "fierce individuality, communal responsiveness, and play, play, play" (360). Through a series of workshops, the participants learned how "to be in the present, truly feel what [they] are feeling, to be honest about what [they] know of [themselves] and the world" (357). According to Osun, the key elements of this aesthetic are "choral work, repetition, layered music, and polyphony." Lastly, these elements come about through the choral work because of "studious listening" (362). Through Osun's description, it is clear that the values of jazz the musical form are embedded in the theatrical form. Namely, the jazz aesthetic in theater means connection to a higher power and freedom. This notion comes directly from the basic tenets of musical jazz. In his essay "Black Music and Social Change," in *Such Sweet Thunder: Views on Black American Music*, Playthell Benjamin asserts, "African American instrumental music became a living example of the American ideal of freedom and equality. The jazz band might well be the only society in the world where these ideals are fully realized" (12). Harjo's mode of expression in *Wings Of Night Sky, Wings of Morning Light* aligns with these descriptors of individuality, community, and creativity. Redbird's journey is directly linked to finding her voice. Redbird's story begins when there are no songs to help her transition through her birth. Her parents have lost their traditional knowledge, which is emblematic of the losses that have plagued many indigenous people since colonialism and continues to do so as colonialist practices persist in the United States. Even though her mother didn't have "cedar or tobacco" (Harjo 2007, 7) at that time, later she passes a pouch of tobacco to Redbird as the young woman leaves for Indian boarding school. Her mother gives her "tobacco and a song," and tells her, "There is power in this song. You have to sing to wake the power up" (16).

Eventually, Redbird finds her voice. She steps up and makes a striking entrance on the night of the "first official Howling Contest," dreamed up by her friend Wind, "who always joked that she was raised by wolves" (2007, 20). Wind commands Redbird, "Let's hear the poetry of howl" (21), but before Redbird can let out her holler, the evening is interrupted by a fistfight. After a long night that includes meeting Sonny, who will become her husband later in the play, Redbird lets out her howl at a diner in the early morning. The scene ends when Redbird asserts, "This is my time." She recalls, "Time lifted up its glorious beaded head and I latched on, and I began to fly" (23). Over the course of this scene, she and her friends each howl, speaking themselves powerfully into existence. Indeed, Redbird's howling/singing wakes up the power within. Through the example of their journeys in this play, other women may find their voices, too. The characters in this play exemplify freedom and expression, and their actions are emblems of personal and social transformation.

Connecting to the jazz aesthetic in a more direct way, we can turn our attention to Harjo's seamless integration of music into her text. In fact, during a radio interview that I conducted at the WMUA-FM studio (University of Massachusetts–Amherst) with Professor Ron Welburn, Department of English, Harjo described *Wings of Night Sky, Wings of Morning Light* as "a healing ceremony of stories and music." Throughout the twenty scenes of the play, she includes story songs that serve as cautionary tales; traditional songs sung in Creek; and songs that underscore the emotional tones in various scenes. There are lullabies and jazz riffs in some scenes; rock and funk grooves in others. This pastiche makes complete sense because Harjo innately understands the connections to poetry and music. In the same interview, she stated, "The poetry of our people has always included music. Sometimes I think poetry feels really lonely without the music."

Harjo is a musician and a poet who says, "I have always heard music with my poetry" (Harjo and Welburn, interview). An award-winning saxophonist, she recorded her rendition of Jim Pepper's "Wichi Tai To" on her NAMMY award winning CD *Winding through the Milky Way* as her tribute to him. She also includes this song in *Wings of Night Sky, Wings of Morning Light*. According to *The Penguin Guide to Jazz on CD*, Pepper's song is a "jauntily haunting theme reflecting his Native American roots" (Cook and Morten, 1183). Pepper, a jazz saxophonist of Kaw and Creek heritage (1941–1992), "based some of his pieces on traditional stomp dances, as well as on Native versions of Baptist hymns, in addition to the ritual chants of his grandfather" (Siegel). He recorded "Wichi Tai To" on the album *Everything Is Everything* in 1969 and on *Pepper's Pow Wow*. Harjo's inclusion of Jim Pepper's music is an important declaration of a much deeper and long-standing connection between jazz and traditional Native music. Professor Ron Welburn states,

> There is a whole galaxy of Native people who have been performing in this music. It's taken for granted that Indian people are not involved in jazz, rock and roll, or various other forms of popular music. (Harjo and Welburn, interview)

At that time, Harjo described her dismay at the striking erasure of Native people's contributions to jazz. She recalled a (then) recent talk by Wynton Marsalis at Lincoln Center in New York, stating, "He completely left out Indian people when he discussed jazz history." She and Welburn then (re)constructed some of this history as they discussed musicians such as Big Chief Russell Moore (1912–1983), who was Pima from Arizona; Oscar Pettiford (1922–1960), born in Okmulgee, Oklahoma, whose mother was Choctaw and father was Cherokee and African American; and Cecil McBee (1935–), Cherokee from Tulsa, Oklahoma. As they reflected on these huge gaps in jazz history that erase the contributions of Native people, Harjo asserted,

> There is a lot of opposition on both sides to consider Indians' contributions to jazz. This notion would require an entire revision of jazz history. Congo Square was an old ceremonial ground and a southeastern tribal meeting space. American music has become so sanitized; the wealth of stories has been left out. (Harjo and Welburn, interview)

Harjo is as much connected to a jazz lineage as she is connected to poetry. In our conversation, she shared that Ernie Fields (1905–1997; trombonist, pianist, and bandleader) took one of her mother's songs and recorded it as an instrumental piece. Harjo described the lasting impression that the image of her mother holding onto the pressing of that recording had on her younger self. In *Crazy Brave*, Harjo's memoir, she describes a scene where she stands perched in the back seat of the family car, her father at the helm and Miles Davis playing on the radio. She writes,

> My rite of passage into the world of humanity occurred then through jazz. The music was a startling bridge between familiar and strange lands. I heard stomp dance shells singing. I saw suits, satin fine hats. I heard workers singing in the fields. It was a way to speak beyond the confines of ordinary language. I can still hear it. (18)

In our conversation, Harjo shared that the first time she combined music and poetry for the 1985 Watershed Records recording *Furious Light*. Shortly after that, she began playing the saxophone. "Someone showed me the G Blues and I started going from there" (Harjo and Welburn, interview). Four CDs later, she is still playing and making visible the connections she felt as a young girl listening to Miles Davis in Indian country.

It is no accident, then, that *Wings of Night Sky, Wings of Morning Light* blends storytelling and music as they have always been intertwined for Harjo. Through her character Redbird, we see a young Muscogee woman reclaim her voice, her sense of self, and her sense of purpose as she reconnects to her family through her grandmother's spirit. Redbird understands her value and her responsibility to her wider community. This play is a reminder to all of us to choose kindness and compassion over fear, greed, and jealousy. When we do so, we find abundance in all that comes our way.

WORKS CITED

Allen, Paula G. *Pocahontas: Medicine Woman, Spy, Entrepreneur, Diplomat*. San Francisco: Harper, 2004.

——. *The Sacred Hoop: Recovering the Feminine in American Indian Traditions*. Boston: Beacon Press, 1986.

Armstrong, Ann Elizabeth, Kelli Lyon Johnson, and William A. Wortman, eds. *Performing Worlds into Being*. Oxford, OH: Miami University Press, 2009.

Baszak, Mark. *Such Sweet Thunder: Views on Black American Music*. Amherst: University of Massachusetts–Amherst Fine Arts Center, 2003.

Benjamin, Playthell. "Black Music and Social Change." In Baszak, 2003, 9–12.

Canning, Charlotte. *Feminist Theaters in the U.S.A.: Staging Women's Experience*. London: Routledge, 1996.

Carlson, Marvin A. *Performance: A Critical Introduction*. London: Routledge, 1996.

Cook, Richard, and Brian Morton. *The Penguin Guide to Jazz on CD*. New York: Penguin, 2000.

D'Aponte, Mimi. *Seventh Generation: An Anthology of Native American Plays*. New York: Theatre Communications Group, 1999.

Darby, Jaye T. "People with Strong Hearts: Staging Communitism in Hanay Geiogamah's Plays *Body Indian* and *49*." In Wilmer, 2011, 155–70.

Däwes, Birgit, ed. *Native Traces: Indigenous North American Drama: A Multivocal History*. SUNY Series. Albany: State University of New York Press, 2013.

Geiogamah, Hanay, and Jaye T. Darby. *American Indian Theater in Performance: A Reader.* Los Angeles: UCLA American Indian Studies Center, 2000.

———. *Stories of Our Way: An Anthology of American Indian Plays.* Los Angeles: UCLA American Indian Studies Center, 1999.

Harjo, Joy. *Crazy Brave.* New York: W. W. Norton, 2012.

———. *Red Dreams: A Trail Beyond Tears.* Audio Recording/CD. Mekko Productions, 2010.

———. *Winding through the Milky Way.* Audio Recording/CD. Fast Horse, 2008.

———. *Wings of Night Sky, Wings of Morning Light.* Unpublished. Permission of the author, 2007.

———. *Native Joy for Real.* Audio Recording/CD. Mekko Productions, 2004.

———. *The Woman Who Fell from the Sky: Poems.* New York: W. W. Norton, 1994.

———. *She Had Some Horses.* New York: Thunder's Mouth Press, 1983.

———, and Ron Welburn. Interview with Priscilla Page. October 2011.

Haugo, Ann. "Native American Drama: A Historical Survey." In Däwes, 2013, 39–62.

———. "'Circles upon Circles upon Circles': Native Women in Theater and Performance." In Geiogamah and Darby, *American Indian Theater in Performance,* 2000, 228–55.

hooks, bell. *Outlaw Culture: Resisting Representations.* New York: Routledge, 2006.

Huhndorf, Shari M. *Mapping the Americas: The Transnational Politics of Contemporary Native Culture.* Ithaca: Cornell University Press, 2009.

———, Cheryl Suzack, Jeanne Perreault, and Jean Barman. *Indigenous Women and Feminism: Politics, Activism, and Culture.* Vancouver: UBC Press, 2010.

Knuebuhl, Victoria Lalani. *The Story of Susanna.* In *Seventh Generation: An Anthology of Native American Plays.* New York: Theatre Communications Group, 1999.

Osun, Omi Joni L. Jones, Lisa L. Moore, and Sharon Bridgforth. *Experiments in a Jazz Aesthetic: Art, Activism, Academia, and the Austin Project.* Austin: University of Texas Press, 2010.

Royster, Francesca T. "Queering the Jazz Aesthetic: An Interview with Sharon Bridgforth and Omi Osun Joni Jones." *Journal of Popular Music Studies* 25.4 (2013).

Sanchez, Sonia. *We a BaadddDDD People.* Detroit: Broadside Press, 1970.

Siegel, Bill. "Jazz and the Politics of Identity: The Legacy of Jim Pepper." *In Motion,* November 4, 2004. Available at www.inmotionmagazine.com. Accessed November 16, 2016.

Stanlake, Christy. *Native American Drama: A Critical Perspective.* Cambridge: Cambridge University Press, 2009.

wa Thiongo, Ngũgĩ. *Decolonising the Mind: The Politics of Language in African Literature.* London: J. Currey, 1986.

Wilmer, S. E. *Native American Performance and Representation.* Tucson: University of Arizona Press, 2011.

Toward the Production of
New Native Theater || An Interview
with Randy Reinholz

Randy Reinholz (Choctaw) is an internationally acclaimed director, producer, playwright, and actor for the stage and screen. He is also the producing artistic director of Native Voices at the Autry, the nation's only Equity theater company dedicated to the development and production of new plays by Native Americans, a company he co-founded with Jean Bruce Scott, his wife and collaborator, who serves as the producing executive director. Native Voices is the resident theater company at La Jolla Playhouse for 2016–2018 and has been in residence at the Autry Museum of the American West in Los Angeles, California, since 1999. In March 2009, Native Voices produced *Wings of Night Sky, Wings of Morning Light* at the Autry, directed by Reinholz.

PRISCILLA: How did you decide to become a theater artist, specifically a director?

RANDY: I was reared in rural America. My father was a faith healer. When his mojo was good, we were welcomed. When it was bad, we had to move. And we had to move often, so I learned to adapt. This informed my perspective on life and shaped my values.

In the small towns where I was reared, there was no urgency to get an education. Most people just got a high school diploma and then got a job in our hometown.

I was a well-regarded high school athlete who went to William Jewel College in Liberty, Missouri, on a football scholarship. While there, I benefited greatly from a coach who told me that the effort I was putting out was not going to be enough. I wasn't big enough or fast enough. I was an athlete, but I was not going to be able to make a career out of it. So, I threw myself into my academic work. It was also at this time that I was diagnosed with dyslexia. Then I met a theater professor who asked me what I was interested in, and I said literature and history. I liked stories. That's what led to my involvement with theater. I studied with Dr. Kim Bradford Harris and Dr. Lois Anne Harris, and they changed my life, opened up new worlds and ideas for me. I am still in touch with them today. At one point, Pavarotti came to perform on our campus, and I was the stage manager for his show. Then the Royal Shakespeare Company [RSC] came to perform. They brought a five-person touring group in the winter of 1983 and, once again, I was stage manager. The play was called *The Hollow Crown*, and I distinctly remember a speech featured in it. It was an adaptation of *Richard II*, and while I didn't fully understand the history or situation faced by Richard, I understood he was speaking from the results of his own decisions and he was destroyed. That moment of that play and speech was unspeakably beautiful. When I met the folks from RSC, I knew that was what I wanted to do—act—tell stories that were real and from the heart. When I think about that time in my life, I think about the RSC actors' advice to me: "Try to meet someone in their fifties and try to imagine doing what they do."

After I graduated from William Jewel College, I auditioned and was awarded a full scholarship to attend graduate school at Cornell University in Ithaca, New York, where I received my MFA in acting. At that time, acting was my passion. After Cornell, I got an internship in acting, and then I earned my Equity card at the Old Globe Theatre in San Diego, California. I had a kind of charm and a boyish look, so at twenty-five I was cast to play eighteen-to-twenty-year-olds. Also, I was not very tall, so I was usually cast as the quirky best friend. I was closer to Johnny Depp than Rob Lowe. Then in 1989, I landed a contract role on *Days of Our Lives* on NBC. I was cast in a few commercials and guest starred on a couple of series. Then I landed a part in a low-budget movie called *Dead Space* with Bryan Cranston in 1991. It was really a charmed moment in my life. I have a great story: I was a poor country boy who earned a degree from Cornell University, and then I actually became an actor in Los Angeles. I also met Jean Bruce Scott, my wife, during that time. She had been on *Days of Our Lives* for three years. After that she was a series regular on *St. Elsewhere*, *Magnum PI*, and *Airwolf* and guest starred on other TV series in the mid-'80s.

By the time I was thirty, I decided I wanted to start teaching. My first full-time appointment was at Duke University, and then I was hired in a tenure-track position at Illinois State University [ISU] in Normal, Illinois. My first semester there, I ended up directing a full production for their main stage. I wasn't nervous because I hadn't directed enough to worry about the short preparation time. The play was *The Imaginary Invalid* by Molière, and I was fortunate to cast a few natural clowns in the production. It all played over the top, and the show was well received for its commedia dell'arte style.

After that, the faculty at Illinois State asked me to bring them a Native play. They knew I was Native because I had filled out the Equity and Diversity Form and identified myself as a Native American. I didn't think it would be too hard to find a Native play, but when I looked up Indian theater at the university library for ideas about what to direct, I only found one play, called *Naked and on a Horse*, and some plays from India. That was in the early 1990s, and the internet was still young. Now, I have directed seventy-five Native plays.

PRISCILLA: What details do you remember about collaborating with Drew Hayden Taylor and Native Earth Performing Arts?

RANDY: I connected with Drew Hayden Taylor, who ran Native Earth Performing Arts, while I was searching for a Native play for ISU. He was welcoming and warm, and he sent me some plays from Canada. I also connected with Bruce King and William S. Yellow Robe, and we did a reading series in 1994 as part of the first year of Native Voices. The Native playwrights were Drew, Bruce, Bill, Joseph Dandurand, and Marie Clements. It wouldn't have happened without Drew's generosity and encouragement. Drew is a gift of a person and a friend. We have produced four of his plays at Native Voices. He knew Tomson Highway, to this day the only First Nations star in theater with a major production in Toronto. Jean and I went to Toronto several times to see work, meet artists, and be part of the center of Native theater in the 1990s. We would go to parties after the shows there, and all the people I had read about who were involved in Canadian First Nations theater were there. Drew was a friend and made us feel comfortable and welcome. Native Earth was the most important Native theater company in North America. Four plays? Who produces four plays together? It must be time to do another. Drew is generous, funny and warm. I am forever in his debt.

PRISCILLA: What plays did you direct in the early years of Native Voices?

RANDY: We were in Normal, Illinois, for the first year, which was 1994. We presented fully staged readings of *No Totem for My Story* by Joseph A. Dandurand [Kwantlen]; *The Independence of Eddie Rose* by William S. Yellow Robe [Assiniboine-Sioux]; *Evening at the Warbonnet* by Bruce King [Haudenosaunee/Oneida]; *The Baby Blues* by Drew Hayden Taylor [Ojibwe]; and *Now Look What You Made Me Do . . .* by Marie Clements [Métis]. We enlisted faculty directors, student and faculty actors, and dramaturgs from across the country. The writers were generous and grateful for the opportunity. After that first festival, William S.

Yellow Robe said to me, "You have to do this again and you have to keep calling it Native Voices." And in 2019, Native Voices will celebrate its 25th anniversary.

In our second year, we presented fully staged readings of *Sitting Bull's Laundry* by William Lang [Lenni Lenape]; *Rose* by Tomson Highway [Cree]; *Only Drunks and Children Tell the Truth* by Drew Hayden Taylor [Ojibwe]; and *Please Do Not Touch the Indians* by Joseph A. Dandurand [Kwantlen]; and we had a full production of *Now Look What You Made Me Do . . .* by Marie Clements [Métis] as the centerpiece. This was 1995.

I directed the 1994 reading of the play and its 1995 production. It was thrilling to collaborate with Marie and to fully realize the power of this troubling story. *Now Look What You Made Me Do . . .* premiered at Illinois State University as a main stage production, and then we were invited to perform at the American College Theater Festival [ACTF] Regional Evening of Scenes in Columbus, Ohio, in 1996. Her poetry and storytelling are stunning. Marie's words touched the audience to their very soul. Some, overcome by the story, left during the performance, while others cheered during and afterwards. I remember a young man, a student and a stunning actor, sitting in the audience motionless after the show. "There is too much of that going on" was his response as I patted him on the shoulder. I am still in contact with that student. It was a gift. Marie's work is stunning, and she should be produced more often.

The theater reviewer for the Bloomington newspaper proclaimed the play unfit for a college campus. He objected to the graphic depiction of domestic violence, sex workers, and transgender characters. He declared that these "ugly" stories had no place in Normal, Illinois. Of course, he forgot to read the front page of his own paper, as that week the headlines reported the tragic story of a local woman who had been beaten to death by her boyfriend at a prominent hotel in town. *Now Look What You Made Me Do . . .* was relevant and important. It pushed the boundaries of "taste" and asked the establishment to see people they routinely ignored as they were being murdered. This critic was also hard on the students' performances. The students understood the problem of his limitations. This review reaffirmed my determination to continue to produce these types of plays. The lesson I learned was that I wanted to be able to ask larger, more difficult questions onstage.

PRISCILLA: How did your move to the Autry Museum of the American West come about?

RANDY: Our first performance at the Autry was *Urban Tattoo* by Marie Clements [Métis] in 1999. It was produced in conjunction with the exhibit titled *Powerful Images: Portrayals of Native America.* If we sometimes felt as though we were fish out of water in Normal, Illinois, we had no idea what to expect when we arrived in Los Angeles to tour the Autry's galleries. We met the programs manager in 1995 after touring the galleries, and actually politely declined to comment on them because they were so narrowly focused on the cowboy narrative at the time. But she wanted to know what we thought, so we sat for over two hours and talked about our observations and the lack of a Native American narrative. After Jean and I gave our feedback on the galleries, the Autry asked us to serve on the advisory board for the *Powerful Images* exhibit. Upon reviewing the plans for the Autry's displays and the discourse around Native Americans for the exhibit, we pointed out that live, contemporary Native people were still missing from the story of the *Powerful Images* exhibition. Mounting a play with Native stories and characters played by contemporary Native people onstage was "evidence" that we were not extinct, that we are here, with issues and needs and much to contribute if we are invited into the conversation. The Autry took that step with us. They wanted to be more inclusive, to focus on diversity, and they met a whole new segment of Los Angelinos. The audiences were thrilled.

PRISCILLA: What similarities and differences do you see in the content that had been produced in earlier years and what Native American writers are addressing today?

RANDY: In general, when an oppressed group gets their voice back, they often communicate about oppression. Many of the early plays at Native Voices were Native American and First Nations stories addressing themes of abuse (sexual, alcohol, violence, and psychological oppression). Those themes tended to dominate the stories.

About ten years into our work, issues of abuse gave way to identity: "Who is really Native?" These issues are front and center in many gaming tribes, since there is "per cap" distribution of profits to tribal members from business ventures of the tribe. Those issues still resonate today in Indian country, though it is much more focused on tradition, language, and culture. Blood quantum continues to be important, and how it is defined and determined varies from tribe to tribe. Each tribe's definition of necessary "blood quantum" for enrollment (which is the government's form of documentation for Indian identity) is better known to both members and descendants investigating their ancestry and rights. The US government's treatment of the indigenous people of this land is highly unusual. It is as if the government is both acknowledging the ethnic cleansing and denying all responsibility for the effects of it at the same time.

Over the past few years, cultural themes of family, untold histories, rule of law, aesthetics, and societal issues (like global warming, sustainability, water rights, and national sovereignty) are front and center. One might say the stories that Native writers are drawing from similar themes as other American and Canadian artists, but from contain an indigenous point of view. Those stories are not solely focused on bad characters from the dominant society or people historically of European descent; rather, on the elements necessary to tell the most compelling stories that foreground Native American, First Nations, Alaska Native, and Native Hawai'ian experiences. Even the plays using history are telling stories that continue to shape contemporary Native American experiences.

PRISCILLA: What is the role of theater and performance in communicating the reality of Native lives to contemporary Native Americans and to society?

RANDY: Native people have used story, oral traditions, songs, and dance to communicate their realities and history for hundreds, if not thousands, of years. Then each tribe, language group, and even clans among the tribes have unique characteristics about how they use these different means of communication and so on. I have some knowledge in some areas, but I do not feel comfortable describing a "pan-Indian" use of these traditional means of passing on and reflecting knowledge. I can say that many of the 566 Native American tribes that were legally recognized as of January 1, 2016, by the Bureau of Indian Affairs [BIA] of the United States, as well as the hundreds more fighting for recognition, are living cultures, each with distinct needs, cultural norms, and aims.

If the question is reframed and reduced in scale to focus on the typical kind of theater and performance we undertake at Native Voices at the Autry for developing and producing new works for the stage by Native American, First Nation, Alaska Native, and Hawai'ian Native playwrights, it is simpler to address. Most of the work we have taken on since 1994 has included scripts the playwrights intended to be shared with a broad audience, that could play anywhere on American stages. Even within these parameters, the role of theater is too big for a short response here. This generation of playwrights is attempting to fill in for the hundreds of years of oppression, suppression, misrepresentation, and media violence that have shaped American conversations and perspectives about what it means to be indigenous. Native Americans, First Nations, Alaska Natives, and Native Hawai'ians have lived through conflicts since the point of first contact. The historical trauma forever imprinted upon all indigenous peoples.

Some plays Native Voices develops and produce confront these violent images head-on; others present the human conditions of Native Americans, First Nations, Alaska Natives, and Native Hawai'ians in more subversive ways. Others depict current issues faced in Indian country and the major legal and social threats to indigenous peoples. Some writers want to present and shine a light on their specific tribal culture and tradition, simply giving the audience a view into their lives.

PRISCILLA: Why was it important for you to create an Equity theater company dedicated to producing plays by Native Americans, Alaska Natives, and First Nations peoples?

RANDY: We had to. It was vitally important to us that Native theater artists be taken seriously by the field. The only way for us to do that was to train actors, stage managers, and directors into a company of artists and to produce Native playwrights under an Actors' Equity Association contract. As Jean and I started reading scripts, first for university and college productions, and then as we shared the scripts with professionals through readings and workshops, we saw the power of gathering artists to focus on plays by Native Americans, Alaska Natives, Native Hawai'ians, and First Nations peoples. We witnessed the power of these stories. Early on, we only had a few ways to encourage other professional companies to produce these plays. With the success of our early productions at the Autry, it was clear there needed to be a company that focused exclusively on producing this work.

Now the goal is to empower other Equity companies and regional theaters to expand their efforts to include Native voices in their seasons and to support emerging Native theater artists by producing their work at higher levels of production. Our perspective has always been that we want to position Native playwrights and theater artists nationally and get them more attention. We want to see Native theater artists working in union houses earning professional wages.

We all have to work together to increase opportunities for Native American, Alaska Native, Native Hawai'ian, and First Nations theater artists in a wider array of artistic arenas.

PRISCILLA: What details do you remember about seeing the early version of *Wings of Night Sky, Wings of Morning Light* at the Public? What struck you about the work then, and led you to direct and produce it?

RANDY: We saw the reading at the Public in 2007. The main image I remember was the kitchen table. It was a metaphor that Joy employed and reclaimed from political rhetoric. Joy framed the table as the place where her family saw, hid from, confronted, and recovered from the issues of her life. The table served as the location where Indian people confronted the historical traumas of this generation.

Onstage, Joy is raw, stunning, kind, and mesmerizing. She has such power, while being completely approachable. She is giving, inviting, and captivating. Yet she does not show off, hoping to get people to applaud for her. She shares from a private, often painful place, sharing a story that is American, and timeless, uniquely personal and informed by the details of growing up Creek in Oklahoma during the era of Patsy Cline. Joy's world is filled with jazz and stomp dance.

Joy also brought together an amazing group of musicians for the reading at the Public in New York led by Larry Mitchell, who we were lucky enough to have continue as a collaborator on the project when we started to work on it in June 2008. Larry, an immensely gifted musician and producer, had just won a Grammy Award for producing, engineering, and performing on *Totemic Flute Chants* by artist Robert Mirabal of Taos Pueblo. As a director, working with a talent of Larry's caliber is like having an extra brain in the room; he always knew just the right thing to do to lift or deepen certain moments in the play.

PRISCILLA: What was it like interacting with dramaturg Shirley Fishman?

RANDY: I loved working with Shirley Fishman. Shirley is a gift of a human being. She can so easily read a script and see the potential, see what is extraneous and know how to ask questions that lead to "what might be." I have worked with Shirley several times since then. I am always bowled over by her compassion, focus, and depth. She is so clear and asks the playwright to pare away anything extraneous. She also asks a lot of "director questions" about how the moments work, what is intended, and what she sees onstage. Her questions lead to changes that deepen and enrich the work.

I think *Wings of Night Sky, Wings of Morning Light* was our first, really intense collaboration. She sat with me after the runs of the show for note sessions that were longer than the actual running time of the show. Sometimes I work with dramaturgs who don't want to interfere, and that is crucial to protecting the authentic voice prized by Native Voices audiences, but Shirley has the ability to advocate on behalf of the writer and still push for theatrical moments onstage. She's not shy.

Writers make their plays better by adding dialogue or cutting extraneous words or scenes to clarify action and intention. Directors realize the world of the play through action and its intersection between actors, design elements, and the audience. The story moves with action and rhythm. Shirley sees all of these perspectives in the same moment. It is a gift to work with her, and I hope more people get to experience her power.

PRISCILLA: Can you describe your experience with *Wings of Night Sky, Wings of Morning Light*?

RANDY: The Native Voices Equity production played for three weeks in Los Angeles at the Autry in 2009. In May 2010, we presented it at Joe's Pub in New York. We remounted it for a benefit performance at La Jolla Playhouse during Native Voices 2010 Festival of New Plays. It was very different in each venue.

The design elements at the Autry were incredible, and that really lifted the show. It was the first full production. The audiences breathed with Joy as she performed. I remember the "giveaway" section as being moving, but it took too long. We decided to have volunteers from Native Voices help with the gifts so that Joy could make it to the peak of the giveaway section. The arc of Joy's performance was captivating. The story has a cumulative effect, with a wonderful punch at the climax of the show. While the story is difficult, Joy's desire to give it an uplifting ending and to empower the listener was always very clear.

The music was so exciting to hear fully produced: Joy blowing the sax and singing, peppering the performance with flute, drum, and rattle. Larry Mitchell was the quintessential "one-man" band, playing a wide array of guitar styles (I think he had four or five different guitars onstage) along with other instruments while he also drummed, recorded, and looped live sounds, and brought in a bunch of recorded cues that he triggered live onstage in unison with the sound designer's effects and recordings.

When we moved to La Jolla, we had little scenery, a few props, and very few production elements. The same was true at Joe's Pub in New York. In those two venues, we saw parts of the show that were not necessary, so trimming the script and streamlining the performance became a priority. Joy's performance instincts helped this process, as anything she consistently forgot became something to question. Joy is a wonderful storyteller, a gift for any director. One of my favorite memories at Joe's Pub at the Public was working with the young lighting designer, who was used to cueing quick changes in support of music acts. He had lots of set cues that worked for the small stage space. As Joy performed, I sat in the house texting lighting looks and sound-level notes to the booth. I really can't remember why I didn't sit in the booth; maybe because there wasn't room. It was fun, and the crew at the Public was fantastic.

Wings of Night Sky, Wings of Morning Light went on to many more performances and productions. Joy has performed the show on her own, and with Larry. They have worked in small venues, community spaces, and grand auditoriums. Just last week, Joy sent a new draft of a new script. We are always looking for chances to support each other and spread the good work happening in Native theater.

I am so happy that *Wings* is now published so that other young Native women, really all kinds of women, can read and speak those words of empowerment, and maybe even see some other performers mount the show. I think of Eric Bogosian's *Talk Radio* and what it meant to my generation of performers. We saw a raw, exciting piece of theater that could be done anywhere. It was topical and muscular writing. The same can be said of *Wings of Night Sky, Wings of Morning Light*. What Joy's work possesses is also beyond compare. I love that the center of her work is so feminine. The power and strength are timeless. The need to hold a family together, even as it shifts and evolves, is such a core piece of the human experience. Joy is a voice for warrior women everywhere. There is also a sense of the eternal in Joy's work. Glaciers move with such force, fueled by years of energy contained by climate and nature. A similar power, the compacting of ideas, lives, and love fuel the work of Joy Harjo.

PRISCILLA PAGE

Imagining a Contemporary
Native Theater || An Interview
with Rolland Meinholtz

It was in the fires of creativity at the Institute
of American Indian Arts that my spirit found a place to heal.

Joy Harjo, *Crazy Brave*

In her memoir *Crazy Brave*, Joy Harjo shares the story of how she arrived at the Institute of American Indian Arts (IAIA) in Santa Fe, New Mexico, at the age of sixteen. It was 1967, and she describes the city as "the epicenter of hippiedom in the West" (86). She decided at an early age that she could not live at home with her stepfather. She also knew that she wanted to be at an Indian boarding school, where she could live and study with other Indian students in "a place where [she] would belong, where [she] would be normal" (82). She learned about IAIA and submitted her application along with her original visual art. Reflecting on IAIA, she writes:

> As we made art, attended cultural events, and struggled with family and tribal legacies, we sensed that we were at the opening of an enormous indigenous cultural renaissance, poised at the edge of an explosion of ideas that would shape contemporary Indian art in the years to come. The energy crackled. It was enough to propel the lost children within us to start all over again. We honed ourselves on that energy, were tested by it, and destroyed and recreated by it. (87)

The school was an innovation founded in 1962 during President John F. Kennedy's administration. Visual artist and cultural educator Lloyd Kiva New and Charles Loloma, his close friend who became a renowned potter and jewelry maker, created the model when they, in cooperation with the University of Arizona in Tucson, mounted an experimental arts program for Native American young people. The resulting success of their experiment shook up the approach to Indian education that had been in place thus far (in the form of Indian boarding schools run by the Bureau of Indian Affairs) and came to the attention of Stewart Udall, then secretary of the interior. Udall, most known today for his enduring commitment to the environment and its conservation, along with his wife Ermalee, urged President Kennedy to bring this groundbreaking approach to the BIA. George Boyce, a longtime BIA official who had headed the Intermountain School as well as the schools on the Navajo Reservation at Window Rock, Arizona, was named superintendent of the newly formed Institute of American Indian Arts in Santa Fe that year.

The Institute for American Indian Arts brought arts education to an Indian school campus that for decades had focused on assimilation tactics and emphasized vocational and domestic training for young Native Americans who had been either forced to attend or sent to live there. These schools operated in a militaristic way, often included indoctrination into Christianity, and were run by bureaucrats through the BIA. Harjo describes it:

> The Indian School world was rife with paradox. Formerly run like a military camp by the Bureau of Indian Affairs, the school had been transformed into a unique school for native arts, like the New York City "Fame School" but for Indian students. Almost overnight, the staff, mostly BIA employees, were asked to accommodate a fine arts curriculum and faculty—an assortment of idealistic and dedicated artists, both Indian and non-Indian. (*Crazy Brave*, 87)

Rolland Meinholtz was one of the "idealistic and dedicated artists" that Harjo met and studied with at IAIA. She describes him as a "master teacher," someone who expected total professionalism from his students and instilled in her an approach to acting that "demanded an alert and knowing body with powerfully developed links to the subconscious" (*Crazy Brave*, 113). She writes about studying dance, storytelling, meditation, and stagecraft, and shares, "Theater gave me the door through which to enter the dreaming realm" (114). Over two days in Fall 2016, I spoke to Meinholtz, who taught drama from 1964 to 1970. This interview highlights his philosophies about art and culture and provides insight into his approach to teaching theater to Native American students and their process toward crafting a contemporary Native American theater movement during a renaissance of Native American culture.

PRISCILLA: Can you tell me about your background and how you became the drama teacher at the Institute of American Indian Arts?

ROLLAND: I guess, the first thing I'd say is I have a fairly decent amount of Cherokee in me, but I was adopted and raised by a completely white family in and around Tulsa, Oklahoma. I had a curiosity about being part Indian, and there is a strange phenomenon in Oklahoma because a large number of people have some kind of Indian blood, but they don't live as Indians. They don't live on reservations, and they don't know anybody else who is Indian. That was my situation. I became a theater student very early on, and I started dramatizing plays and stories when I was three, and I just kept on doing it forever and ever. Then, I went to Northwestern University, and from there I went on to do my graduate work at the University of Washington, in the directing program. I started that program in 1959, and when I finished, I was looking for a job. My boss in the Washington program knew that I was part Indian for some reason, and when he saw the Santa Fe job description, he said, "Hey Rolly, I think this might be something for you, uniquely."

I responded to their query, and after talking on the phone, and doing all the usual dances we have to do, I was invited down to IAIA, and the person who took charge of me, showed me around, and interviewed me was Lloyd Kiva New. I was hired under the music department, and I worked with Lloyd because drama and dance were in the same program as music. There were eighteen different faculty teaching in the arts for three hundred kids, and then there were academics teaching English, history, science, and that sort of thing.

Lloyd and I became very close, maybe because we were both Cherokee, I don't know. He was terribly interested in drama and the possibilities of Indian drama, so the theater program was really a special baby for him. We worked directly together, and we started unintentionally bypassing Jim McGrath [head of the arts program] and Louis Ballard [head of music]. There probably was some resentment about that, but basically it worked because Jim and Louis were big about it. Lloyd was the one with stimulating ideas, and he was willing to get you juiced up and then take a step back. He had vision about what was possible, but he didn't try to spell it out. He was looking for somebody who could do that. He gave me a little test when I arrived. He handed me a copy of Diné Bahané, the Navajo myth of creation. It was an old version, and it was beautifully printed. It sort of looked like a one-of-a-kind edition, printed solely out of love. It was quite different.

PRISCILLA: Can you tell me about this myth?

ROLLAND: The Navajos conceived of pre-lives for people. We were down below this earth. People would find a hole in the sky to climb through and come into a new world; the Hopis believed this new world was the fifth world. Changing Woman, a character in the story, was created in the fifth world, which is where we are now. It was ruled by terrible monsters, and anytime people tried to come up and be in the fifth world, the beautiful world, they would be eaten by these monsters. The other world was dark and damp; people weren't happy, and they were hungry. It wasn't a nice place, and something had to be done. Changing Woman was given an urge to seek out the Sun. She thought the Sun might be a person like herself, and so she climbed up a mountain and was actually impregnated by the Sun and, in the story I read, she had twins. These magic twins grew up to be creatures who went around the world killing off the monsters. So, during my interview for the job, Lloyd handed me this story and said, "How would you dramatize this? What would you do? What would it look like?" I don't remember much of what I told him or did for him, but we both got very excited about it, and it was a wonderful thing for me. This story fit in perfectly with my interests and the studies I'd been doing. It got me the job, and it continued to fascinate me. It stayed with me during my entire time at the institute.

Three years after that, I started working on a play of my own based on that legend and a Hopi creation myth in which the people come up and meet the Hopi god of death and life. He's the god of both. He's called Masawu, and they work in agreement with him so that he allows them to come up and be a part of this world. That became the play that I wrote called *Journey to the Sun*. I self-published it with another one of my plays called *Black Butterflies* alongside works written by my students at the institute.

PRISCILLA: Can you describe your interests and influences in theater?

ROLLAND: I studied theater with Alvina Krause as an undergraduate at Northwestern, and she was very important in my art and life. She wrote about the creative process and developed an expanded approach to teaching acting at Northwestern. I have a picture of Alvina and a picture of Lloyd on my wall here, and I consider them my artistic mama and papa.

Somewhere along the way, I became aware of the work of Jacques Copeau and the Théâtre du Vieux-Colombier in France in the early twentieth century. His innovation was really a return to the basics in terms of acting and staging. He was famous for using a bare stage in his productions. He was influenced by

Shakespeare's Globe Theatre. He also developed a system of acting that was particularly geared to using the body to speak more than the voice does. I found all of his ideas very exciting, and I wrote my dissertation on Copeau's work. I was also studying French theater at that time, and I made it a point to see as much French theater as possible, particularly French theater in the French language. I did a thesis performance of a play by Jean Anouilh, and I used what I learned from Copeau in that production. I also had a very firm background in Stanislavsky's method. In his system, the actor discovers and explores their inward impulses regarding the dramatic context and the individual character they must bring to life. When the work is stylized, as in Molière or Shakespeare, the actor steps into that stylized world, but the core of their reality, the inner basis, steps with them. Such an actor develops an exquisitely detailed sense of the forces (both cultural and theatrical) that shape their character's life. Then they adopt their character's outer circumstances and, using their inner work as a foundation, build the overarching style, the structure of why and how their character does what they do. Copeau, and the French movement, excited by Stanislavsky, took his method a step further by developing physical training for their actors, which gave them the tools to successfully communicate the innermost lives of their characters through physical presentation that many felt revelatory in its precision and poignancy. I believed that Native American theater would profit from this same approach.

I was also very interested in Greek drama, and through Greek drama, I became interested in Indian drama—that's not American Indian, I mean from India. Kathakali, the classical Indian dance form, particularly caught my eye and ear. I was most interested in early theater that did not use the proscenium stage. The way dance was used in India to tell stories was utterly fascinating to me. Balinese shadow puppetry and dancing was also interesting to me. I brought Copeau's influence and these additional interests in theater from around the world with me to IAIA.

PRISCILLA: How did you learn about Kathakali and Balinese shadow puppetry? Did you study those forms in college as well?

ROLLAND: I learned largely by reading about them. Though while I was at the University of Washington, I had a wonderful experience with the Manzo Nomura family, a Noh theater group from Japan. We actually saw them perform, and they demonstrated specific techniques for us. It was just remarkable, the artistry of this family. The father and son were key to the company, and the son was a tremendously virtuosic actor. He was wonderful to work with and to watch. He was exciting to be with, but Manzo, his father, was like the codification of a lifetime in the theater. He glowed with the love of the theater. He possessed all of the virtuosic techniques of his son, but these were not his raison d'être; rather, these were seemingly effortless tools that he could use when he found it appropriate. Through his performance, the deepest spiritual meaning of the work manifested. It was a truly remarkable experience for us, as students, to be in his presence. They also directed us in the staging of a Kyogen play. After we cast the play, they told us that they wanted us to perform it in Japanese, but we couldn't quite swing that. What touched me the most happened as we prepared for our final dress rehearsal and performance. These great artists knelt on the floor and costumed us. They tied the ties on our costumes, and they shared the history of the form with us. It was so moving and utterly remarkable.

PRISCILLA: What was the drama program like when you arrived at IAIA in 1964?

ROLLAND: When I first got there, I didn't really know much about what I was going to do. I had never taught people who weren't theater people to start with, and these young people were just kids—they were actually high school kids. Almost all of them had been raised in tribal circumstances, and that meant that we had a healthy complement who came from towns and cities as well as from reservations. They were Indian in a way that I had never been in my life. I remember I would have nightmares about how might I connect with these kids. I would think, "What's it gonna be like? Will they think I'm just a stupid old white man trying to get them to do stuff?"

Well, that all quickly went away. They were wonderful. The first group I taught were the most wonderful students I've ever had in my life. I also learned a great deal from them. Their values are different. Human relationships are thought of differently. Family is thought of differently. Quickly, it became obvious to me how incredibly important grandparents were to these young people. They also seemed to be one step closer to creativity than we were, than most people are, especially those who came from strong cultural networks. It was less common to see that in the young people who came from cities like Los Angeles or Chicago. I'm not quite sure why, you know, because a lot of people say baldly that American Indians are intrinsically artistic. There's a germ of truth to that, but I think it's wrong-headed as a generalization. They're not necessarily more gifted artistically than anybody else, but they're much closer to artistry; it's not such a journey to get to full creative expression as it is for the rest of us sometimes. And so that was a wonderful gift to work with, because we had an exciting idea, and they got excited about it, and wonderful things really did happen very quickly. It was just amazing.

We began working, and before too long, we developed two projects. In my playwriting class, two kids were trying to write about their grandparents, so I began working with them and hoping something would come up for us. In acting class, I introduced those students to Shakespeare's *Macbeth*. I quickly learned that there was a story among the Nootka Indians on Vancouver Island that was extremely close to *Macbeth*. This story had some wonderful differences, too, that were typical of Indian culture. We all got excited about it. From the very beginning, Lloyd guided us with his vision: "We believe American Indian theater to be different than European theater." We asked, "If it is different, then how would it be different?" This was the foundation of our work.

PRISCILLA: What do you remember about the school?

ROLLAND: The library at the institute was extremely good, and it was useful for this work. It was a small library, but it had wonderful Native American materials. I researched anthropological papers, archaeological papers, and stuff you wouldn't find anywhere else. I began doing massive research. I'd just come out of graduate school, and I was in the mode of using a library in very creative ways for my theater work. It was terribly important to me to have powerful visual material available. There were tremendous stores of photos and paintings and other such things about Indian life starting in about the 1880s. The photographs by Edward Curtis were incredibly important to our work. The details that you could see and really get a feel for what it was like to be alive when Native people *were* Native people and not so heavily influenced by the European culture that was invading their country. I remember back to our development of the character of the grandmother in the play *Black Butterflies*. That character came from a Curtis photograph of a little old lady who was bringing home a huge pack of firewood on her back. But, the most outstanding thing to me about the school was that it didn't have a building or even a space within a building that was a theater. None.

PRISCILLA: That's a challenge. [Laughs.]

ROLLAND: But the rest of it was positive. One of the ways the school did things was that when the kids would create art, it would *be* somewhere where you could go to see it and interact with it. Art was everywhere you went. Every building had art studios. Kay Wiest taught photography; I'm not sure she had a studio per se, but she had a developing room and a place where she taught. They had several painting ateliers. The artists Otellie Loloma, Leo Bushman, and Allen Houser had a shed with their studios together. There was art everywhere you went. Pots, pictures, textiles. Seymour Tubis shared his printmaking and his printing on fabric. Josephine Wapp displayed beautiful traditional weaving, another form of textile art, on the walls of her studio. It was tremendously important. You could not get away from it. On the campus there were statues and fountains, and we had an art gallery in the administration building. So the kids knew if they produced things, that everybody was going to see them and they were going to be talked about; this was all part of the community of who we were as artists. I've never been in a school like that, and I felt like I was on fire. It was really special. There were eighteen professional artists on the faculty. One of the qualifications was that we needed to be actual professionals in our fields. You know, I was probably the weakest one there, by the way. [Both laugh.] It was great to be able to *talk* to these people and share ideas and have them see what you were trying to do, and they'd listen. And they didn't always comment, but sometimes they got excited. You could see they were excited, and you'd say, "Well, you know, that's neat." That was nice to have that kind of excitement and that kind of reinforcement.

PRISCILLA: Yes, that sounds really wonderful.

ROLLAND: I like that it was a residential program for the kids. It helped the focus. They didn't have the distractions of home or the hangouts of wherever they lived. Everybody lived here at IAIA, they ate here, and they worked here.

PRISCILLA: Did that help build a sense of community among the students?

ROLLAND: Absolutely. They also had a wonderful counseling system on campus. We didn't limit the kids at all. All they had to do was say, "I want to be there," and they could come. If they had a portfolio, fine. If they didn't, fine. As long as they said they wanted to be there, they could come. We had kids who were so troubled we couldn't keep them sometimes. We had one boy who came, and he was kind of interested in theater, and I had hopes for him. He looked like he might be a wonderful Coyote person, I don't know; he took too much of whatever drug he was on, and he went down the line of the academic building and broke every double window on one side of that building. It was really spectacular. He did these flying tae kwon do-type kicks and just knocked out every window. Well, of course we couldn't keep him here. I wish we could've—that kind of fury has got to go somewhere.

PRISCILLA: Exactly.

ROLLAND: Most of the kids were really sweet and wonderful. But they often needed a great deal of help. Indian life is no bowl of cherries. Through the counseling program, we were able to actually deal with the rougher side of their life and give them an important plum. We would say, "You can be a creative person. You can use this juice to make things that matter and are beautiful, expressive; things that are important to you and the rest of the people in the world." We created a wonderful, wonderful atmosphere. It was the most amazing thing in my life. Northwestern was a pretty exciting place too, but it was nothing like working at the institute.

PRISCILLA: I wanted to also ask you about Father Staudenmaier. Joy writes about his profound influence on her in *Crazy Brave*, and she credits him as "the first person to talk about the soul to [her]." Could you tell me what you remember about him?

ROLLAND: He needed to complete fieldwork as a part of his graduate program, and he asked to be sent to the Institute of American Indian Arts. He became tremendous friends with the kids because he could really talk to anybody. He became a moral buttress for almost everybody. We had tough times because some of the kids were fighting their addictions, and sometimes there were fights between the tribes. We had kids from every tribe in the country, including Indians from Hawai'i and Alaskan Inuit. We also had Native people who don't consider themselves Indian. So there were disagreements and problems. We had a very large Pueblo group of students because we were so close to the Pueblos, and we also had a large Apache representation. There was a large Sioux contingent largely because of the Catholic fathers, who would seem to do more than others to get those kids to come to government schools. They would say, "Here's this school, don't you want to go? They won't restrict you. They'll take you if you want to go, and it's supposed to be a wonderful place. Why don't you go and get out of here?" Father Staudenmaier was really wonderful dealing with such things, and giving us a primer on what was going on. He helped us understand that we needed to pay attention.

Later, when we toured our productions with the students, he became our main connection to home for us. He really took care of us while we were away. He opened many doors for us and kept other doors closed that might have been troublesome. He was a wonderful guy to have on your side, and he was certainly on our side. He was a good friend to me personally, and he was very supportive during a later time when there was real personal trouble developing in my family.

PRISCILLA: Did the theater students have much experience as performers prior to coming to the institute? How prepared were they to work on a production?

ROLLAND: I think most of them would have had a least one pass at something, but it was not very significant, in my experience. Now, Joy, she looked pretty raw, scared of failing, but she had mountains of earnestness, not only about theater but everything in her life. There was a lot of training that had to go on there.

My program really started to take shape in the second year, and I felt very strongly that I had to give the students a theater education that would not embarrass them in front of anybody else in the theater. I wanted them to know who Shakespeare was, who Chekhov was, who Aristophanes and Sophocles and Euripides were. And what commedia dell'arte was. I wanted them to know all of that and to be able to do a great deal of it. So we spent the fall and a little bit of the winter working on theater, as it is commonly understood. I wasn't interested in Broadway, though we did do one play from Broadway that the kids loved deeply, and they did terribly well with it. We performed *A Taste of Honey* by Shelagh Delaney, and that was right down their alley. Those young people really understood that play, and it was a wonderful production. The kids at the school, of course, were the bulk of our audience, and they would keep coming back to see it. Time after time they just came back to see the show because they understood it and loved it so much. By that time we had a proper theater to do our work.

PRISCILLA: What was your theater space like?

ROLLAND: It was an open stage arrangement, not terribly different than Copeau's Vieux-Colombier. There were more similarities to it than to the Globe. It was a bare stage sticking out into an audience that was severely raked in front of it. The seats were almost at a bleacher rake. It created a very intimate feeling. We quickly decided that dance would be an integral part of any Native American performance that we created. The idea of Native American theater didn't exist in those days, but we decided that dance would be at the center of everything we did. We hired Rosalie Jones, dancer and teacher, and the kids would spend half of their time in theater and then they would spend half their time in dance. It was a very close relationship.

In the second half of the year, we experimented with dance and plays our students wrote. And since we said that dance was central, we had to ask, "How do we incorporate it?" Ceremony is also very much a part of Native American theater. It's one of the pillars: dance, ceremony, and a relationship with the spiritual world that's not in terms of anybody's specific religion necessarily. Spirits are important regarding what happens on this earth. I became interested in that kind of theater before I came to the institute. Early on, I was somewhat uncomfortable with that idea. It was through my connection with the Japanese Kyogen group that I learned about Noh theater. That was my first experience with theater that concerns itself with the spiritual more than the literal. And through that, I gained a comfort with that idea. At the institute, we decided that the Native theater we were creating would place that same value on spirituality, and we began to work on how to do that.

PRISCILLA: What were some of the productions you directed, and what do you remember about them?

ROLLAND: We did a production of *Uncle Vanya* by Chekhov; we did a production of *Oedipus Rex* by Sophocles. Actually, the first Greek play we did was his *Elektra*, and the students really enjoyed that. They knew what it meant to be angry in a situation that had been terribly unfair to them. That play really reached their hearts, and they did beautifully with it. You would think that high school kids would make fools of themselves, but they didn't! It was just magnificent. The choral part of the play helped us introduce the idea of dance in the theater. Well, it wasn't exactly dance we did, it was actually marching, but we got them closer to being able to express themselves with their bodies that way. Rosalie began doing dance pieces that were simply unique and powerful. That production opened the door for us to do our own stuff.

PRISCILLA: What was Santa Fe like in the mid-1960s? Was there a thriving arts and culture scene?

ROLLAND: Yes, there was traditional ceremonial theater going on all around us. That was one of the glorious things about having the school where it was. There was this tremendous web of theater occurrences. You have to put quotes on the word "theater," I suppose, because the purpose was primarily ceremonial not theatrical, but it *was* theatrical as well. Whenever possible, we would grab a bus with the kids, and we'd go and see a ceremony at Cochiti or ceremonies at Santa Domingo or at Taos. Some of the most important events we attended were the Shalako ceremonies at Zuni. We actually went through the whole ceremony there. It was an all-night ceremony. It was thrilling and very moving. Lloyd and I made a point to go to the Long Horn ceremony at the Zuni. Then Otellie and Charles Loloma opened a door for us; it was just unbelievable. They were the reason we were able to go. Lloyd and I were invited to go to the Hopi Bean dance, and we were permitted entrance into the kiva, which as far as I know has very seldom happened for anybody else. The Bean Spirit appears at the crack of dawn at the edge of the village, and then she comes into the village with the sun rising behind her. It's wonderful theatricality going on there. She holds bean sprouts in her hands, and this is in February. This is how the Hopi emphasize the idea that life renews itself; it goes away and it comes back. The people sprinkle corn meal on the kachina, and they take the sprouts back to their homes. They grow them into plants, and they do whatever they want to do with them. There are performances all day long and into the evening. And what they did [laughs] for us—I'm pretty sure it was deliberate—was they did a great deal of spoofing white people who go to Florida for vacations. It was just a hoot. [Laughs.] Of course it was all men, and they had lots of wonderful cross-dressers, and they did what they considered outrageous for women of the tribe. It was just a funny and wonderful performance.

There is something else I remember. We came in and saw how they rehearsed. The elders coached the performers. Do you remember when I described the Kyogen performers robing us and how that was so beautiful for us? I can't describe for you how moving that was to see the same ritual at Hopi. You know, I could practically write a whole book about that experience.

PRISCILLA: You would take students to see these different kinds of ceremonies and different performances?

ROLLAND: Yes, whenever we could, we would take them. We also took them to many ruins that were all around us. One of the most important to me was

Chaco Canyon. I went with Lloyd originally, and then I took students there. I've been back since several times. It's just an amazing place. It's a huge settlement. Chaco Canyon is probably the ancient population center of the United States. They may have had, well, nobody knows, but somewhere between twenty and forty thousand people in this area, and their architecture was incredible. It's very beautiful, and Pueblo Bonito was three stories tall. They'd have these huge kivas; that's one reason why this was so important. The kiva is essentially an architectural theater space for the staging of ceremonies. The biggest one is at Chaco Canyon, and I believe it is about sixty-five feet across. There is a big circle for performances much like the ones we saw with the Hopi, only we were in a twenty-by-twenty building there. We also visited the Aztec Ruins National Monument in Farmington, New Mexico. It is close to Chaco Canyon. They have a completely reconstructed giant kiva there, and it's a thrill to see in every way. The acoustics are incredible. They designed the space, which consisted of smaller rooms that were all connected to the central, great room. I describe this place in the article that I wrote for Birgit Däwes's book, *Indigenous North American Drama* (2013). In that piece, I share the discovery about sound design that Lloyd and I made when we visited there. This confirmed what we wanted to do with Paolo Soleri Amphitheater at our school. Lloyd invited Soleri, an Italian architect who taught at Arizona State University, to design an outdoor space for us in 1965. Lloyd, Charles, and I gave our input based on the various types of ancient and modern theater venues we knew about. Soleri was a leader among architects who proposed that architecture and ecology can and should work together.

PRISCILLA: As you introduced these ceremonies and these spaces to the students, did you ask them to reflect on their experiences? How did they bring what they learned into the creative process that you were developing with them?

ROLLAND: Mostly, it just happened. We did have conversations, particularly about dance and the role of dance, and we reflected on that. We particularly felt we had achieved something. Like with any project, we had a lot of chaff—things that we tried and that didn't work, and we'd say, "We're not gonna do that again."

The first show that we did was *Moqwina/Macbeth*, and we masked everybody one way or another, either with heavy paint on the face or with actual masks. For the three witches, we used a Bokumus. The Northwest Bokumus is a spirit that has a grudge against mankind. The spirit goes off in the forest, and it tries to lure particularly important people into the forest with it and lead them to madness. We translated the witches in *Macbeth* into something familiar to Native Americans. After doing that, we looked at it and we talked about how we felt face-painted masks were too much somehow. The students and I realized that what was more typical, as we looked at Northwest ceremonials and the Pueblo ceremonials around us, was that the mask was only used for a specific character who had real spiritual power. This is how the Bokumus is portrayed. It signifies that the character is sort of extra-human. And so that became our practice. Most of the people did not wear masks, but for instance, in *Black Butterflies*, the character of the grandma was masked. She was a good and special person to the two young people in that play. One of the things I reflect on with sadness is that the way we worked didn't continue. Hanay Geiogamah started his theater company around 1970. As far as I know, he took a bunch of our students and, with Café La MaMa as their sponsor, created the American Indian Theater Ensemble. That was after I'd left the school. When Hanay got the kids, their work went in an entirely different direction. I don't know, it's like, what we had done went totally by the wayside.

PRISCILLA: Do you mean that the elements of ritual and ceremony and those sorts of performance practices went away?

ROLLAND: Yes, as far as I can tell, those elements weren't very prized at all. This was during the time when Indians were protesting for the first time. The occupation at Wounded Knee happened at that time. I think the protests just grabbed the forefront, and whatever we had done did not seem to have ways of dealing with those situations. When I think about what happened to our ideas about theater and what could have happened, that's one of the areas that I ruminate on the most.

PRISCILLA: There didn't seem to be a way to reconcile the social protest with the ideas of ritual and ceremony in performance?

ROLLAND: Yes. Now, William Yellow Robe, who I taught at the University of Montana, he has done some work in that area, and he has begun to try to develop some of the ideas. I do remember that in one of his plays, he used a sort of proto-dance and a choral effect for the characters. It happened near the end of the performance. It brought that scene to vivid and memorable life.

And it just kills me that the people up in Indian territory in North Dakota right now who are protesting the Dakota Access Pipeline aren't using theater. There ought to be theatrical performances up there! Performance is a part of protesting and making community together, and they're not bringing it in. It just drives me nuts! It's absolutely what we were about.

PRISCILLA: I can totally see your point. Can we talk about some interesting things that happened when you toured *Black Butterflies*? Joy mentioned some memories from Port Angeles in Washington. Can you tell me about that?

ROLLAND: Yes, we performed two pieces at Evergreen College: *Black Butterflies* and our main piece, *Ianius*, written by Monica Charles. She's Klallam Indian, and the reservation is about ten miles outside of downtown Port Angeles. Monica was raised in third world circumstances; she knew desperate, desperate poverty on the reservation. Lloyd met her when he was visiting that area, and he just was so appalled that he made a special effort to make it possible for her to come to the school. Her mother refused to help her and even tried to stop her from coming, even though Monica was old enough to come on her own.

The play is autobiographical for her. In it, she shares how it was that she came to the Institute of American Indian Arts. One of the main reasons that she came was because of an uncle of hers who had always taken a special interest in her, but he was also a man who was deeply censured by his tribe because he was something of a drunk and a rascal. He could never settle down to ordinary life. Monica explored this contradiction of feelings about her uncle in her writing. She loved him so much, and yet he was labeled as no good. The play is about making peace with that, and showing her own people that he was extremely valuable to her and that he mattered. He's the main reason she decided to leave the Port Angeles area and to come to our school. Her uncle is the main character in the play. Well, we arrived at the theater, and we were excited to be there. We were really looking forward to presenting the play in Monica's hometown. As the audience started to arrive, we realized that it was overwhelmingly Native people coming in. It was practically Monica's whole reservation in the house.

PRISCILLA: Wow.

ROLLAND: *Then* who should come in but five minutes before the play started, but her uncle himself. Monica came up to me and she said, "My God, he's here." She was afraid of what he would think about seeing himself in the play, and she was practically a nervous wreck! He came right down to a seat in the middle and in the front. Everybody in the community, every single person in that audience knew he was there within five minutes of his arrival. There was an electric zing in the air; you could just feel this energy go through the whole theater. We performed the play, and it seemed to be well received. Afterwards, Monica went down and talked to him about it, and he was fine. He asked if he could meet the cast, particularly Keith Conway, the actor who played him. For the character of the uncle, we used a mask. Do you remember I told you the special characters in the drama, the ones who are special people with spiritual connections, were always masked? The uncle's character was masked in our production. Her uncle was fascinated by that. He talked to Keith, and he seemed to like the play very much. Then he took the mask and looked at it. Slowly, a big smile spread across his face. He licked his teeth and looked at the mask and said, "Jeez, you're no good!" [Both laugh.]

One of our ideas was to develop a theater *for* Native people, and if other people like it, that was fine. But we saw our work as a place *for* Native people. I remember when we were in another town where we did the show for people from another reservation, and they stayed after the show. They were so excited to see something about themselves and about their ways of life that they held us up for about thirty minutes. They wanted to talk to us, and it was a wonderful feeling.

PRISCILLA: Can you describe more of your artistic process and how you collaborated with artists from other disciplines?

ROLLAND: One of the most helpful things that happened to us was that we were asked to create two different festivals [the American Indian Performing Arts Exhibition in 1965 and the Festival of the Arts of Indian America in 1966] at the Department of the Interior in Washington, DC. In preparation, I traveled all over the country to meet with Indian peoples and to select groups to be in the festival. I went to Florida and worked with the Seminole tribes, and then I went to New York and met with the Seneca people, and then the Apache people in southern New Mexico, and the Navajo at Chinle, Arizona, and the Alaskan people in Haines, Alaska. We auditioned groups to be in our show, and we had to figure out how to include them. Most of them didn't have shows per se. They had dances, and we talked to them about how to use what they had. Lloyd and I worked together on both shows to develop a framework for these different pieces so that they would flow together. The first festival was a really lovely piece, and the second one was a lot more adventurous. We really developed a script for the second one that was based on the Sipapu stories of the Hopi. Louis Ballard wrote the music for the piece, and he's a tremendously talented composer. He proved to be very difficult to work with. [Laughs.] That's one reason why the show was not quite as lovely as it might have been. Both of these shows really got me out and aware of what Native performances were like all over the country.

We had visiting artists come in to the school to teach. Rosalie Jones was the first guest artist, and we were very impressed with her. I had seen her work at the University of Utah, where she was in the master's program and had been working on using Indian materials in creating modern dance pieces. She was just a beautiful fit in terms of what she was doing with her art and life and what we were doing. We ended up hiring her in the second year, and we worked together very successfully. She worked with us on how to physically express the unique spirituality of Native Americans. During her time at IAIA, she also did innovative work with floor patterns. We knew that dance was important to Native Americans in terms of how it was laid out on the floor. We made great connections with the audience because of that kind of work. She also paid close attention to sound patterns such as rhythmic stepping, the stomping of feet, clapping of hands, thumping of bodies, and chanting. We explored all these things to find out what we could use and what was right. She also worked out how to visualize the spiritual relationships we explored in our work. She developed one dance from the Sioux Sun Dance ceremony. Maybe you've seen pictures of the dancers that peg sticks of bones into the skin of their chests. Then they dance against the thongs, which are wrapped around the pegs on one end and tied to the top of a pole on the other end. Their dance maintains a tension between the dancer and the center pole until the dancer achieves spiritual ecstasy and passes out. Rosalie's choreography reflected the overall image of the ceremony. She used a simple rope to connect one Sun dancer and an imposing woman, costumed in a white deerskin, who represented the center pole.

The show *Deep Roots Tall Cedars* ended with a major dance. We used screens designed by faculty member Neil Parsons in it. The dancers carried screens with Northwest designs on them. The screens were on poles that came down and touched the earth, and they could lift them, pound them, rotate them, and interlock them into visual patterns. This was another way that we worked with different artists.

Later, Rosalie introduced us to Barry Lynn. He was a private dance instructor in Salt Lake City, where Rosalie went to school. She developed a friendship with him, and she worked closely with him. He spent half of the school year with us, and he was really wonderful to have because he was very influential in helping us develop our understanding of how dance could ground our work. The soul of dance, for us, was its connection to the earth. Barry really understood that idea, and we improvised together. We had long conversations, and then he actually developed studies with the students where they would try out various ideas of what we might do. Barry was very much trained in the Martha Graham style, and sometimes Graham just didn't go with anything Indian. But, it was all really delightful to try. He choreographed a duet for men and some small group pieces that proved to be exciting and provocative for our work. He worked on the challenge of the repetitive nature of Native American dance. Because it is so repetitive, it can become boring in theater. As ceremony, it can go on for hours. At Pueblo villages, the dancing goes on all day. There are artistic reasons for doing that, but our problem was that we didn't have all day to achieve our effects. We also wanted to appeal to not just a Native audience, but to other audiences as well. We wanted to create excitement within ritually exciting things. We all worked extremely well together, and he advanced our thinking. Barry gave Rosalie a great deal of confidence in what she was doing and attempting.

Charles Weidman, one of the fathers of modern dance, came to work with us, and he had a great impact on our work, too, even though he only came for a long weekend of dance workshops. Rosalie spent time with him beforehand, so he was hip to what we were going after. He developed a piece with our students that looked something like the kind of flowing serpentine rapid group movements that Mark Morris does these days. It was lovely. I also remember that he would bring humor into the work, and that was tremendously helpful when we started doing our comic shows.

Tone Brulin, a Belgian playwright, actor, and director, was another person of real influence on us. He had studied extensively with Grotowski in Poland, and he was with us for a full academic year. He'd originally been brought to Antioch College, and they found they just couldn't use him there. They called us up and said, "We have this embarrassment of riches; can you do something with him?" And we said, "Sure!" [Laughs.] He taught us a sequence of yoga moves that he learned from Grotowski's company. The sequence is called "The Cat," and it had an immediate and profound beneficial effect on our training. I have used it ever since then. Tone also worked with Bruce King in developing his play *To Catch Another Dream*. They worked on it for about three months, and then we produced it in the winter of the last year I was at the school.

Tone taught us how to make use of the bare stage, especially with naturalistic material. We learned how loudly one, precisely chosen, prop could speak to an audience. This helped us tremendously with Bruce's play that was set in urban Chicago. We learned how to use our bare stage to create that place with only a few props and a single set piece. We really made it all work.

Terry Allen was the creative writing teacher, and she was a willing and very helpful comrade. She had all the kids who wanted to write in her class. We had lots of strength coming from her program into ours. Monica Charles started writing in her class. Terry was a very talented teacher that I was sure glad to have as a colleague.

Henry Gobin was an assistant teacher to Jim McGrath in the beginning, I think. He was a former student, a very recent former student, and Lloyd assigned him to be my right-hand man when I first started during that real shaky period that I mentioned earlier. He was ideal. He really was a tremendous help. It was through him that we became aware of the outstanding theatricality of the Northwest Indian tribes, which led us to the *Moqwina/Macbeth* performance. That was done with Northwest Indian masks and costumes. Henry was the assistant director for the first Washington Indian Festival that we did for the BIA. He was a young man of a great many ideas, and he was excited about what we were doing in the theater program. He was somebody who was just really nice to have around. He was a potter and a visual artist.

Charles Loloma was also on faculty, though he wasn't there much. He was one of the most sought-after jewelers in the world when he was alive, and he's even more so today. I can't believe how much his jewelry's gone up in value. He is one of the great artistic names in the history of Hopis. His home was in Hotevilla, Arizona. We spent time there on several occasions.

Charles was also a great potter, and he became utterly fascinated with china during the time he was at the school. He worked with porcelain on a big wheel down in his studio. One day I walked in, and he was throwing a porcelain pot. It was at least eighteen inches tall, and it was ten or so inches across the flange at the top. He was trying to take it down to the china thickness, which is, as you know if you have any china, very thin indeed. When you throw something like this, it has the tremendous capacity for falling down. It's wet clay, you know. It was amazing to watch him. He'd just reach in with one hand while he had the other hand on the outside. It looked like he was nursing . . . I don't know how to describe it. And, of course, his focus! It was tremendous.

He was very strong, and he wanted his pottery to be as beautiful inwardly as it was on the outside. The shape of the pot was absolutely vital to him. The beauty of his process overwhelmed me. I got pulled into watching him create the space within the pot. The combination of his focus, his skill, and his daring was very much a part of it. When he finally finished, he turned and looked at me with the devil in his eye because he knew he had defied everything. The piece was huge, and I was drawn into watching him create that enormous space within it.

PRISCILLA: Would you say that what you saw in his focus and in his creativity was something that you wanted to translate into theater?

ROLLAND: I don't know that I thought about it at the time, but yes, it was a transfer of his art coming to my art, I hope. Charles was probably much more of an artist than I ever thought of being, but he certainly gave me many gifts. He and I were getting a little high one night and he brought over a wonderful bottle of almond-flavored tequila. It tasted a good deal like a good medium-weight sherry. It was incredibly smooth, and we were having a great conversation. All of a sudden, he grabbed my knees and he put his knee outside of mine and he kind of locked me in to a knee embrace, then he leaned over to me and began breathing loudly and deeply. He was missing a couple of teeth, and some of the other teeth had big gaps in them. I was very conscious of the whistling of his breath, and then suddenly he barked, "Don't you UNDERSTAND, Rolly? How important breath IS to the theater, to EVERYTHING." I don't think he said much more than that. In and out, breathing and showing me. Giving, taking, receiving. It's the whole basis of everything. I don't know if those were precisely his words, you know, but it was just an electric moment that only could come from somebody like Charles. Once again, an elder teaching a protégé.

In our theater practice, we began using breath, particularly in Tone's cat exercises. It was very logical as with all the yoga work, that breathing was very important. We began to see breath as a connection between us, and I would have the actors breathe together in interesting ways as we prepared for our performances. Sometimes we would put our heads together radiating like a sundial and then breathe until we were perfectly in sync together in the same rhythm and at the same time. This was very important for us.

PRISCILLA: What are your observations about the differences between Native American theater and non-Native theater? What differences have you experienced when attending plays?

ROLLAND: Well, any play begins from where the audience is when they come in and sit down in the theater space. There is usually the anticipation of the performance, the quieting down when performers appear, and then it's almost like we sit up a little straighter to see what's going on. Most theater shares this. However, we, Indian people, like to extend that time by including some kind of processional. At powwows, for instance, the dancers make a grand entrance to a very slow, beautiful song. Everybody who participates in the powwow will come in and move through the powwow circle several times and then find their places and make final preparations for what they're going to do. That's really universal. When people come in to any of the Native performances, there's a sense of low conversation and warmth because of the fire, which is at most of the performances. There is a sense that something significant might happen. I think we share that, but it's more geared to beauty, happiness, something that will touch you, your life, that that's somehow more expected, I think, in a Native audience. Because of its ceremonials and rituals, there is a sense of going to church in the theater. Another observation I have is that Western drama seems to be built at the base of mountain. In the beginning, you arrive, and then it begins its ascent. You climb and you climb and climb until you *reach* the top! And then somehow, very quickly, you are magically, once again, at the bottom of the mountain without too much peril. That seems to be the kind of thing that's going on in European drama. In Indian performance, I would shift the image to that of a glass being filled very slowly with a beautiful liquid, and then through movement and time, the glass is full. That's the difference. Native performers and audiences are patient. It's good because something really lovely is happening. Oddly enough, the audience feels emptied, almost in a sense that a flute is empty after you play a beautiful tune on it. Is it really empty? You know, if you just heard this beautiful thing come out of it? Is that really empty? Or is it a quivering space? I don't know. There's something romantic about it. [Both laugh.] But then maybe it's an inner buzz that points to something important. That's woven into my heart, my being.

There is another difference I want to share. I remember seeing O'Neill's *Long Day's Journey into Night* about forty years ago. I had to stand for the performance; it was standing room only, and it lasted three hours, easily. Maybe it was four hours. It was one of the ultimate experiences of my life. I loved the playwright and the actors. By the time it was over, my partner and I were just struck dumb. We couldn't say *anything*. We could barely walk, but we did, and the only place we wanted to go was to a bar and get a big shot of whiskey. We could not talk until we'd had almost all of that whiskey. Then we began talking for a long time. It's very difficult to describe, but the Indian feeling would have been different. After seeing the play, you would not be struck dumb, you would feel lighter, you would walk lighter, you would feel happy. Even with serious drama, you would feel energized, not depleted. I think we came close to doing that with our work at IAIA, but I can't say we ever really achieved it. I would have loved to achieve that feeling. It's out there; I know it can be done.

PRISCILLA: That's really beautiful. Now, I want to ask you about the time when the school changed from an art institute to a college? What were your impressions of that change? What do you think of that change today?

ROLLAND: First, I should tell you about a rather important evaluation visit from José Limon and Martha Hill. Limon stands with St. Denis, Graham, Weidman, Cunningham, and Ailey as a leading light in the history of modern dance. Ms. Hill was the director of modern dance at Julliard for many years. They were brought to our campus as a critique team. I invited Father John Walsh, the widely known and respected head of drama from Marquette University, for the theater portion of the evaluation. The idea was to assess our performing arts program, identify what we might do to improve, and think about what might be developed in the future. They observed our performances and classes, and then we made remarks about our work. After that, we had a formal discussion with the evaluators. All three were thrilled and extremely complementary of our programs and the achievements, but unfortunately this process set the stage for great damage to be done to the program.

PRISCILLA: Oh no! Why was that?

ROLLAND: Well, Ms. Hill felt that Rosalie, while good, in the long run was not sufficiently an exalted teacher to base the future of our program on. So she said, she's gotten you off to a good start, but you really need somebody else to look long into the future.

PRISCILLA: Wow.

ROLLAND: Of course, being young and full of myself, it never occurred to me that she might have, and perhaps even wanted to, make the same comment about me. Anyway, Ms. Hill and the other people in the program, *our* program, chiefly Jim McGrath, put a lot of pressure on me, and I'm ashamed to say that I gave in to it. It's one of the worst decisions I've ever made in my life. That's how we came to separate from Rosalie, and that's how things were killed off. Rosalie was absolutely a key person in our program.

I'm trying to skip over some of the grunge details. Juan Valenzuela came to us around that time. Oddly enough, Rosalie had him lead a workshop on our campus as an artist in residence. I think he was there about a week. He was slick, and he gave wonderful workshops. The students loved working with him, and he seemed perfect for us. So after finding some pretext for letting Rosalie go, I went to him and talked him into working for us. Why he agreed is an interesting subject for speculation. He and I did not work well together. He did not see theater and dance as a marriage. He did not believe in the existence or possible creation of a unique Native American theater, and the day-to-day grind of teaching a small group of students was not his cup of tea. Now, that's my view. I don't know if anybody else on earth would hold that view, but I'm telling you honestly the way I felt about it.

During that time, Lloyd and I also began a concerted effort to gain financial support to run our program during the summers in the Soleri Amphitheater that had been completed by then. We made a money trip to Oklahoma to try to raise funds from universities in Indian states with Indian programs. We were certain that neither the BIA nor the Department of the Interior were going to do anything for us. This was during the Nixon administration. The funding situation from that era was beyond belief. We had been essentially on the same budget for four years, and of course, the funding was less every year. The dollar amount was the same, but because of inflation, which was much more significant in those days than it is now, we had less. I couldn't see any hope. I think Lloyd was really feeling the stress, too. Our search for money to support the summer program was a total failure. It astounded me how little people were interested in supporting that. Despite the many strong points we talked about and what we had already achieved, it didn't seem to make any difference. It began to look like we might lose our financial support altogether if we were not able to don the robes of being a college program, rather than a high school.

Lloyd saw the writing on the wall and put all of his efforts into transforming IAIA into a college. At the same time, I was in personal crisis with my wife and family. It just looked like I needed to get out of there, so I did because I didn't see the possibility of any improvement. There was also a tension between us and other BIA schools. It seemed like the other schools envied us. They seemed to think that IAIA got everything that they couldn't have. And they wanted to know why. They seemed to ask, "Who were we? Why were we so special?" We were spending something like four thousand dollars a student for the year, in those days, and they got something like twelve hundred dollars for the year. And of course, we would say, "Well, you're the ones who are being wronged. We're getting what is necessary to do a good job. Look at what we've done. You guys have had 70 percent of your kids never make it beyond high school, or even finish high school, and we're up to 80 percent of them who finish high school and then 50 percent who go on to college." There was a reason for that, you know. We had positive proof of success. We had students like Kevin Red Star, Earl Eder, Tommy (T.C.) Cannon, and Larry Ahvakana. I could just go on and on and on about the kids who have made names for themselves, who became somebody. Jane Lind, a girl from my program, went on. And Joy, and all these people. They have done important work and made real contributions. Joy, as everyone knows, is an internationally known and loved poet.

So Lloyd supported the change from a high school to a college. I talked to him years afterwards, and I know he was not entirely pleased. He never felt at home with the school after that. For a time, they were not terribly friendly with him either. I think they reevaluated that. Later, Joy taught there. She can tell you about her experiences. William Yellow Robe really wanted to be the drama person there for the longest time, and finally he just said, "It's not worth it." I don't know the college very well these days. No one there has ever contacted me except one time, and then suddenly they just stopped. They were talking about having an interview with me like you're having now, and it just never happened. I had the impression they had little or no knowledge of the achievements of the school that preceded them.

PRISCILLA: That all sounds really difficult and even disappointing. I really appreciate getting to know more about you and your work at IAIA.

ROLLAND: Thank you. This has released a great deal for me. I think I have some writing to do now. Nobody is able to tell the story that I can tell. I feel it's so necessary. I feel like I want talk to Joy and see if we can't get together to really talk through a lot of the memories so we can pass this knowledge on. There's so much more that has to be done before I lose it. [Both laugh.] You know, Joy inspires hopes. She is an artist who has the attention of the world for what she does.

NOTE

For further reading, see "Coyote Transforming: Visions of Native American Theatre" by Rolland Meinholtz in Birgit Däwes's *Indigenous North American Drama: A Multivocal History* (State University of New York Press, 2013)

WORK CITED

Harjo, Joy. *Crazy Brave*. New York: W. W. Norton, 2012.

PRISCILLA PAGE

Learning to Be || An Interview
with Joy Harjo

PRISCILLA: Can you describe your earliest theater performance?

JOY: If my earliest theater performance is a performance onstage, it was a ballet and tap recital when I was five years old, on a stage in Tulsa. As we practiced ballet in preparation, I performed without knowing why I performed. My mind was a ball of questions. I wondered why these movements? Why this style and manner? And for what purpose? I could not ask anyone these questions. They would not come out of my five-year-old mouth the way that I was thinking them in my much older mind. But tap was a different matter. It was like blues and jazz. I felt it in my bones. I loved rhythm. And I loved the red satin outfit that made me want to move. I was more familiar with the music. It was how I lived every day in my ears.

I wasn't the kid upfront, the star, the twirler. I was quietly charismatic. I still have photographs. However, my first acting part was in kindergarten as a Pueblo girl grinding corn. I still remember the corn-grinding song. We performed for our parents. I had to kneel on the floor and pretend to grind corn.

I continued to have roles in plays all through elementary school. The most memorable was as a witch for a Halloween play. I was popular in it for my improvised witch laugh that made its way all around the school. In sixth grade, I was the understudy for the fairy godmother part, the second role after Cinderella in the operetta of the same name. I was one of the shyest in my classes always, and when I nearly failed speech class for refusing to speak, I forced myself to speak enough to get a passing grade. I usually made As and Bs, so to get a D was unacceptable. Theater, however, was a different creature. I could become someone else; inhabit a character, another place and time. And, as my teachers said, I had a voice that carried. I felt magic on the stage. It held possibility. I was lucky to even have theater in my elementary schools. (I went to three different elementary schools in Tulsa.) We children had an opportunity to experience stagecraft. Theater serves human development in many ways.

The first professional or semiprofessional performance was when I was in high school at the Institute of American Indian Arts. I signed up for theater with Rolland Meinholtz after hanging around the theater group in the fall and assisting with stagecraft for a production of Shelagh Delaney's play *A Taste of Honey*. In the late winter, Meinholtz began assembling a show around a play by postgraduate student Monica Charles, *Moqwina*, and one of his plays, *Black Butterflies*. I was given a female lead, and Jane Lind had the other. Though I suffered from stage fright (which became nearly debilitating when I started my band Joy Harjo and Poetic Justice), I felt more at home on the stage than I had felt anywhere else in my life. It is also the poet and musician in me who thrives in liminal back roads. It is a place of all possibility, where vision happens, where metaphor lives.

PRISCILLA: Who encouraged you to write poetry and to perform?

JOY: Poetry was in my life because my mother loved poetry in books and the poetry of song lyrics. I associated poetry with books, and song lyrics with guitars and guitar players. Music came into my early life primarily through the radio, and through the players who came over to jam and rehearse with my mother. This was before I was seven. After seven, this life broke apart. On the radio, we heard Elvis Presley, Buddy Holly, Nat King Cole, and lots of country including Hank Williams, Patsy Cline, and Johnny Cash. I was in a tire swing when I heard "Ring of Fire" blasting from a car radio. My mother preferred slow, heartbreak ballads. She sang and wrote them. She also recited poetry she learned up through her eighth grade schooling. She quit. Wearing the same dress every day made her an object of bullying. She remembered William Blake poems, some Tennyson. She gave me books of poetry, and I began finding poetry to read on my own.

I wrote a poem in eighth grade English class because our teacher wanted submissions for an all-state anthology. We also wrote stories. My story got honorable mention. I do not remember what I wrote in either form. At Indian school I wrote a foolish limerick, and was a prodigious note passer. And then tried my hand at some lyrics for the school's rock band. I didn't know what I was doing and those lyrics never went anywhere, though I did go-go dance onstage with the band a few times with my friend Belinda Gonzalez. I never took a creative writing class at IAIA. I've always loved dance, and because we were working hard on a production, which involved dance in our performances, we were in the dance studio two or three hours a day.

It wasn't until my first year at the University of New Mexico that I attempted poetry. My first semester, I majored in premed and minored in dance. Elizabeth Waters was a renowned modern dance figure, and I was referred to her classes by dancers. By second semester I was back in studio art, and I had met the Acoma poet Simon Ortiz and we were living together. He was the poet. I stayed up all night painting and drawing. My first poems were very derivative. They were immature and naïve constructions from some vague notions I had about how to put a poem together. When I realized that I was a witness of times that were different from previous generations, when I heard very few voices of Native women in political meetings, and I wanted to hear them, that's when my voice showed up and I had to follow it. The summer of 1973, when my daughter Rainy was born, poetry began taking over my art practice. That was also the summer of Wounded Knee; and the Kiva Club, the UNM Native student organization, was politically active. I was a very committed member.

I began performing my poetry almost as soon as I started composing the poetry that would define me. My gift emerged around the time I was pregnant with my daughter Rainy. I wouldn't exactly call what I did *performance*. It was me standing at a podium, tightly holding pages of poems so the audience couldn't see my face, and I couldn't see the audience. I suffered deeply from stage fright, was very insecure, and doubted my authority to speak. I believe both the audiences and I were taken by something larger than me, the voice of the poetry. I had to keep following it. I had no choice. Speaking the poems was a necessary part of the gift. I learned with every opportunity I was invited to speak my poems. I was encouraged by my two beloved teachers at the University of New Mexico. David Johnson: my first poetry workshop was with him. I found a doorway in with his inclusive and warm style of teaching. He was an active poet and took us, his students, along to readings. We also read. Gene Frumkin was my second teacher. He was more serious, but his manner was inclusive. Under his tutelage we students wrote, attended readings, and were also encouraged to take part. Due to the efforts of the creative writing faculty, we always had an exciting slate of visiting poets. They included Galway Kinnell, Anne Waldman, and Ai, to name a few.

In my last year at UNM, I gave my first professional reading. My fellow undergraduate poetry student Terry Boren and I were featured as part of the UNM English Department Reading Series. That spring I was accepted into what was considered the best writing workshop in the country, the Iowa Writers' Workshop at the University of Iowa. My first book, a chapbook *The Last Song*, was released by Puerto del Sol Press in Las Cruces, New Mexico.

I left late summer from a place of much support and encouragement to a high-powered writing program where I found no close mentors. I was akin to the small-town girl going to the big city. The poet William Matthews was friendly and understood lyric. Donald Justice was kind to me. I had the sense that no one really got what I was doing, or they thought that it wasn't compelling. Or our end goals were different. Yet what united us was the need, as artists, to write the best poetry. I wouldn't have made it through without Iva Roy, a Meskwaki Native woman who took the very few Native students (only seven in all of the University of Iowa) into her home and fed us, took care of our spirits. Nor would I have completed the program without the companionship of Sandra Cisneros and the rest of our Third World Writers group, and the fiction writer/artist Dennis Mathis. Very early on, I got the message in the workshop that performance in poetry was to be avoided. To perform poetry was to cheapen it. The word should be without emotional entanglement but stand on the two feet of craft and technique. I can see how this philosophy of disengagement morphed into deconstructionism of the late eighties and nineties . . . I felt lost my first semester there.

PRISCILLA: As a young person, who were your favorite artists (of any form)?

JOY: I loved art and wanted to be painter. In every house we lived in during my childhood, we were accompanied by the charcoal drawing of two horses running in a storm by my grandmother Naomi Harjo. I liked to enter into the image and feel the storm, feel the horses, the shock of the first lightning strike. In childhood when the thunderstorms would begin, I would run to the door to greet them. I was not afraid. I learned to be afraid.

I often lingered over images whose creators I did not know. I understood at a basic level how color and line translated emotional fields. I could feel the personality of the artist, their disappointments, their aspirations. In elementary, junior high, and high school, I became familiar with the art of Picasso, Cézanne, Monet, Manet, the pointillists, the impressionists, and the photography of Man Ray. One of my favorite paintings was *The Sleeping Gypsy* by Henri Rousseau. It came close to the quality of my dream world. Gauguin's French Polynesian paintings pulled me in. I was also very familiar with Oklahoma Indian artists like Jerome Tiger.

Television was young when I was young. My favorite shows were the variety shows that showcased dancers, like the *Ed Sullivan Show*, the *Jack Benny Show*, and *Red Skelton*. I loved watching the June Taylor Dancers, who were featured on the *Jackie Gleason Show*. I watched Dick Clark's *American Bandstand* and *Soul Train*. I imagined being one of those dancers. Martha Graham was a revered figure for me. I was terrified of her fierce countenance, but her intelligent mining of mythological emblems and symbols fed me.

Music was everywhere: my mother's original songs and her singing, Nat King Cole, Elvis Presley, the Beatles and the British Invasion artists, Johnny Cash (especially "Ring of Fire"), Miles Davis (before I knew he was Miles Davis), Jimi Hendrix, Motown artists, the opera—especially *Carmen* by Bizet—Joan Baez and other folksingers, Taos round dance songs, and later stomp dance songs. I also loved the song "Amazing Grace."

I came up through my first elementary school in Tulsa, Burbank, with a strong arts program. I'll never forget my first art teacher, Miss Wastier. (I'm not sure of the spelling of her name, but it was pronounced "wast" [like wasp] "tier.") She was like a wasp. She was slim and precise, with large black glasses. She had a sting. Her rules were exact and were meant to be followed absolutely. Most of our classroom of second graders was terrified of her. I was too, but we got to make art in her class. And we did. I always walked into her classroom with a mix of excitement and terror. We also had music. I learned to read music and was one of the children often called on to sing. And there was a dramatic performance in every class every year. I was in most of them. One of the teachers told me that I was picked because I had a voice that carried. I loved performing in plays because I could become someone else, not the shy, terror-ridden child who wouldn't speak in class. I liked the magic of being onstage. Most of the plays we performed were from a repertoire of plays written for elementary school children. In sixth grade, at my third elementary school, I was chosen as the understudy for the second lead in *Cinderella*. It was an operetta, so I was required to sing. I still remember the songs. I never had to step in, but I loved being part of a production, the kind of space theater makes of dramatic storytelling. I knew that I loved theater, but I did not have a thought of being an actor or singer. I wasn't outgoing like other students. I didn't have the constant of music lessons or a family who came to see my performances. My father was gone by the time I was eight years old, and my mother worked two or three jobs.

PRISCILLA: Who are your mentors, and how did your relationships with them form?

JOY: I have acquired some outstanding mentors along the way. They include the writer Ishmael Reed; poets Adrienne Rich and Audre Lorde; fiction writer, activist, and poet Meridel LeSueur; and many others.

And my previously mentioned creative writing mentors were some of the most influential, but one of the most pivotal mentors of all was my drama teacher, Rolland Meinholtz, at the Institute of American Indian Arts. When I arrived at Indian school, I was on the verge of disappearing into the streets. And no, I wasn't streetwise, quite the opposite. I had nearly lost the will to live. When I got accepted into the Institute of American Indian Arts, it sparked my heart. I applied with drawings and was accepted. I was alive again, and far away from a very abusive stepfather.

I remember hanging out during rehearsals for a drama production of Shelagh Delaney's *A Taste of Honey*, a perfect selection for our student body. The British playwright was eighteen when she wrote the play. As I mentioned earlier, I assisted with stagecraft, and I loved being inside theater society.

As we prepared our schedules for second semester, one of my friends said she was signing up for drama. I remember saying this: "I will never get on a stage." I signed up anyway. It was there I began learning under Rolland Meinholtz, our drama teacher. Being onstage and learning stagecraft engendered happiness in me even as it challenged my stage fright and raised up all those pools of self-doubt I had tended within. I felt exactly who I was and didn't have to make excuses or run away. I was chosen as a lead in a play, and became one of the only two high school students of a show that was mainly comprised of postgraduate students. We studied every aspect of stagecraft: set up lights, made masks, honed our bodies with dance even as we learned how to fall. I really needed that one: how to fall. We learned how to get up again. We rehearsed until sometimes two and three in the morning, and were allowed later morning hours.

I knew Meinholtz absolutely believed in me. He believed in all of us, and whipped together a group of renegade Indian students from all over the country into a semiprofessional company, one of the first all-Native theater companies. I can imagine what it must have taken, in terms of time and resources, to accomplish this in a school that was essentially a Bureau of Indian Affairs school. He had a mentor in Lloyd New, a visionary Cherokee artist who headed that school through its most influential and famous years. Meinholtz treated us as professionals; and we were, though there were bumps in the road. I was informed years later by a previous dorm staffer that there was a plan at work to put me in custody of the school, because it was obvious my stepfather was abusive. When the letters went to our parents to ask permission for us to tour our show in the West, which was quite an accomplishment to be included, my stepfather overrode my mother and denied me permission. My mother stood up to him for what was probably the first time ever in their relationship, and I was allowed to go on tour. He didn't talk to her for almost two months. Meinholtz mentored many young playwrights, like Monica Charles, who wrote some of our plays, and William Yellow Robe.

PRISCILLA: What were some of your opportunities to share your poetry with the public?

JOY: I have performed my poetry all over the world, from Amsterdam to India, to all over the Americas, Egypt, and nearly every European country. I have performed as a solo reader, with a full band, with one or two other musicians. I took up saxophone when I was nearly forty, around the time I started the band Joy Harjo and Poetic Justice. I learned to play saxophone for *Letter from the End of the Twentieth Century*, my first album. I began learning to sing (or should I say remembering to sing) on *Native Joy for Real*, my second musical album. My next album, I learned flute. I will also be playing some of the guitar and bass parts on my newest project. *Wings of Night Sky, Wings of Morning Light*, my first full-length play, came about as I performed onstage with my band, Joy Harjo and the Arrow Dynamics Band. I would speak between songs. And as I would speak and connect songs, I thought, why not put together a show with a dramatic arc, with a full band, why not make a play?

That was how I started this play. I didn't want to be bound by my very personal story; rather, I wanted the freedom to move, so I fictionalized the story. I began writing, and inserted some of my songs, and then I created others to go with the story. I had been working with the guitarist/producer Larry Mitchell, and asked him to be part of it. He created synth pads and helped with transitional instrumental music to get us from one dramatic movement to another. The ambiance that his music created really helped to make the show. When people would ask what he was working on, he liked to tell them it was a one-woman show.

PRISCILLA: When and where did you learn the most about writing and performing?

JOY: It is difficult to say where I learned most about writing and performing. I am always learning. I took it into my pores, as all children do, in childhood. I watched country swing artists perform at concerts and in my home. I watched and listened to my mother, to what was presented in the classroom. In fourth or fifth grade, our class was taken by bus to hear a classical music performance of *Peter and the Wolf.* Our music teacher prepared us for the experience in advance. We were taught the instruments, what voice each instrument represented, and we were prepped on the story to enrich our experience. It was one of the most memorable classroom experiences.

PRISCILLA: What are some of your biggest challenges as a performer?

JOY: In space there are so many possibilities. The artist, whether a poet, playwright, saxophonist, or actor, is involved in a call and response with the unseen, with the Great Potential. The biggest challenge, for me, perhaps, is vulnerability. Allowing myself to step into the known—but to do this knowledgeably, you need all your practice, your craft, your technique, and in a sense, you have to un-know your knowing. Letting go is a big one. To allow yourself to fail is another part of it. Stage fright is another. I have many stage-fright stories, most involving saxophone. When you blow saxophone, you cannot hide behind a few pages of poetry. It is a loud, even obnoxious instrument, though it can be nuanced and even tamed to be expressive in a classical European manner. I believe the saxophone prefers blues and jazz—then it can let loose.

I once wrote: *The saxophone is so human. Its tendency is to be rowdy, edgy, talk too loud, bump into people, say the wrong words at the wrong time, but then, you take a breath all the way from the center of the earth and blow. All that heartache is forgiven. All that love that humans carry makes a sweet, deep sound and we fly a little.*

I identify, then, with the saxophone.

Once I was tapped to open a show of women drummers in the Bay Area with a poetic opening. I asked to play sax. They gave me an eight-bar solo. During rehearsal, I did exactly what I had been rehearsing in my mind: I played badly. There's nothing like the thudded silence after musical failure. It has a decay that will send you running for home with your tail curled between your legs. I could feel everyone wondering why I was being allowed to play. I decided to return to my hotel room and pack up my bags and skip out. I went back and began packing. Then my spirit came and talked with me. I realized that I had to reset my practice in my mind, to playing successfully. I went to the next rehearsal. I wasn't bad, but I didn't nail it. The night of the performance, I was out of my mind with terror. But, I watched as the singer Faye Carol sang and entertained the audience. My spirit told me, "She's not obsessing over perfection. Watch and listen to her." I understood that she was just listening to the music. She was absolutely present, and loving what she was doing. She was in it.

That shifted performance in me. I pulled off my little solo. I didn't fly, but I didn't shame myself either.

I've learned that when energy comes before performance, we often equate it with fear. It's not. It's a gift of energy coming to us to help us out. This lesson helped when I had to perform my *one*-woman show (with a guitarist!). I had to memorize the whole show, and then I was having problems sleeping because I was so wound up. Sleeplessness is a major cause of forgetfulness. So to use the insomnia, I imagined that the show was a story being told in the early hours of the morning, before dawn, after the people had been in ceremony all night. That helped.

PRISCILLA: How did you feel the first time that you decided to play the saxophone in public?

JOY: My first performances with saxophone were in Tucson about 1989. I collaborated with the keyboardist singer/songwriter Keith Stoutenburg. We played my original poems with music crafted around them, the precursor to my Poetic Justice stuff. I was terrified to play, but just being inside the music compelled me. One of my favorite performances was to improv on soprano sax with Keith and a bass player. We were background music for some event that Keith was asked to do. We just . . . played. I didn't struggle with stage fright for that one. The next one, I did. I brought in Keith and Michael Davis, the bass player for MC5. We started performing and then I froze on my horn. I put it away and didn't perform again with it that evening. I was so ashamed at what I deemed my most absolute failure. I hide behind stage and didn't want to go out and meet the public after. My spirit had a talk with me. Very logical. My spirit asked me, "Do you want to play saxophone? You don't have to, you know." I answered, "Yes." "Then play. Play every chance you get." So . . . I did. I've learned, too, that it helps if I am prepared.

PRISCILLA: Who are your role models today?

JOY: John Coltrane
   Miles Davis
   Toni Morrison
   Lorraine Hansberry
   Um Kulthum
   Charlie Hill
   Johnny Depp
   Wilma Mankiller
   Jim Pepper
   Big Chief Russell Moore
   Tribe Called Red
I think Pura Fe and her blues slide guitar is one of the most exciting things happening in Native performance today.

PRISCILLA: If you were starting a career as an artist today, how would you do it?

JOY: It's different these days. There's internet and social media. Anyone can write and produce music and put it out there. It's affordable. Publishing is different. There are lots of online magazines. But the basics are the same. Practice. Study. Connect with mentors (in body or spirit). It is important to challenge yourself. Stretch. I would be much more savvy in my overall plan. Promotion is everything, but you must have the goods. Taking care of the quality and vision of your art is primary.

PRISCILLA: What is one thing you wish you had known much earlier in your career?

JOY: I wish I absolutely believed in myself. Too often I allowed insecurity and self-doubt to waylay me. I didn't trust my spirit or my gifts.

PRISCILLA: What inspires you to continue to write and perform?

JOY: The same things that have always inspired me—to follow mystery, to hear and see beyond what I ever thought possible, and the stories and songs of my ancestors. I have specific goals on the horn, with my voice, performing and writing projects. I am learning how to listen, always. I want to play, write, and be that which brings forward a fresh vision for my people.

PRISCILLA: What are your next goals as a performer?

JOY: I just turned in the book of my musical, *We Were There When Jazz Was Invented*. I will write the music, and I want to get this play produced with all the elements fully realized onstage. I've gone from a one-woman show to one with over thirty characters. I want to write and produce a bluesy jazz Native album of music. I'm working on a historical memoir that may be written as poetic oratory. And I will get a band together in Knoxville, where I now live. There are lots of musicians here. And I started a young Native women writers' group with the Cherokee writer Mary Kathryn Nagle.

PRISCILLA: If you could go back in time, what would you say to your younger self about creativity and performance?

JOY: I would say, just be yourself. And give gratitude to those who have gone before.

ACKNOWLEDGMENTS

MUSIC CREDITS FOR
Wings of Night Sky, Wings of Morning Light

Larry Mitchell: Guitar and synth pads, sound design, funky loops, moods, transitions, and inspirations throughout the show by Larry Mitchell

Joy Harjo: Rabbit Is Up to Tricks,* Spirit Helper Lullabye, Flute Courting Song, Mother Protection Song, Nothing I Can Say (from) Had-It-Up-to-Here Round Dance,* This Is My Heart,* Falling Falling (with rhythm track by John L. Williams), Shining Persons Arrive Here Healing Song, Goin' Home,* I Want to See the Children Play

Wynema Jewell Baker Pickett (my mother): A Long Time Ago, lyrics adapted by Joy Harjo

Jim Pepper with Joy Harjo arrangement,* Witchi Tai To

Traditional Mvskoke Trail of Tears song

*From the album *Winding through the Milky Way*, c Mekko Productions, Inc 2008, produced by Larry Mitchell

Thanks to Silvia Mauther for Production Photos for *Wings of Night Sky, Wings of Morning Light*

Thanks to Ken Van Wey, Program Specialist at Indian Arts and Crafts Board for assistance with the 1968 IAIA theater photos.

JOY HARJO THANKS / MVTO

Rolland Meinholtz, for your teaching, your love of theater and drama, and your belief in the Native students at the Institute of American Indian Arts. We began to believe in the possibility of the power of story, personally and universally, which is one and the same.

Betsy Theobald Richards, whose idea it was to situate the play around the kitchen table, and who is one of Native theater's biggest advocates and supporters.

Randy Reinholtz, for directing, for believing in the story of Redbird, in the
    possibility of Native theater, all the while running a program and teaching.
Jean Bruce Scott, for all your support and love, ever and ever.
Shirley Fishman, for your tough insistence on the best of story making and
    revision.
Native Voices at the Autry, the whole crew for a good run and support—from
    great snacks and assistance when I couldn't sleep, to lighting, set design,
    sound, all of it.
Charlie Hill (RIP), my unofficial coach and spirit lifter upper during the run.
Loren Khan and Isabelle Kessler, for listening.
Suzanne Tamminen, for your patience and ongoing belief and hard work on
    behalf of American literature.
Priscilla Page, for helping me carry the vision.
Owen Sapulpa, for your love, support, and belief in me.

PRISCILLA PAGE THANKS

UMass–Amherst Native American Indian Studies colleagues Ron Welburn,
    Alice Nash, and Lisa Abrams for their advocacy and support during this
    process; Claudia Nolan for transcribing Rolland's interview and read-
    ing early drafts of the chapters; Joy Harjo for her healing words; Brettney
    Young for her love and understanding; and my partner in all things, Glenn
    Siegel.
Special thanks to Ryan Flahive, archivist at the Institute of American Indian
    Arts, for researching theater production details.

The playwright and co-editor, JOY HARJO, was born in Tulsa, Oklahoma, and left in 1967 to attend high school at the Institute of American Indian Arts in Santa Fe, which was a Bureau of Indian Affairs school mostly for high school students. She graduated from the University of New Mexico in 1976 with a BA in creative writing. Harjo has published eight award-winning books of poetry. Her most recent collection of poetry is the recently released *Conflict Resolution for Holy Beings*, which was on the short list for the Griffin International Prize and was named the American Library Association's Notable Book of the Year. Her writing awards include the prestigious Ruth Lily Poetry Prize from the Poetry Foundation for lifetime achievement; the Wallace Stevens Award from the Academy of American Poets, also for lifetime achievement; a Guggenheim Fellowship; and the New Mexico Governor's Award for Excellence in the Arts, among others. Her memoir *Crazy Brave* won several awards, including the PEN USA Literary Award for Creative Nonfiction and the American Book Award. She has published two award-winning children's books, *The Good Luck Cat* and *For a Girl Becoming*.

Harjo has been performing music with her poetry since the early 1990s, when she founded the reggae-tribal-jazz-rock band Joy Harjo and Poetic Justice. Her first album was a spoken word CD, a spoken word classic *Letter from the End of the Twentieth Century*. This CD featured her saxophone playing and was called "the best dub poetry album of North America." In 1998 she went solo and produced *Native Joy for Real*. On this album she began singing. Poet dynamo Bob Holman says of this album, "This is the work of a poet at the top of her powers, whether the driving force is voice spoken (crazy beats of 'The Last World of Fire & Trash,' poetry of 'Hold Up'), voice sung (the incredibly moving 'Grace'), or saxophone (moving from the Native unisons to a Hip-Hop beat in 'Reality Show')." Harjo's next album began her work with producer and rock guitarist Larry Mitchell. *Winding through the Milky Way* won many awards, including a Native American Music Award (NAMMY) for Best Female Artist of the Year. Her most recent release, also produced by Mitchell, is *Red Dreams, A Trail Beyond Tears*, which has won the attention of such critics as Paul Winter, who has said of her music, "Joy Harjo is a poet of music as she is a poet of words." Harjo was featured on HBO's *Def Poetry Jam*, Jim Lehrer's *NewsHour*, and a Bill Moyers series on poetry Harjo's "one-woman" show, *Wings of Night Sky, Wings of Morning Light*, which premiered at the Wells Fargo Theater in Los Angeles in 2009. Harjo is at work on a musical, commissioned by the Public Theater, *We Were There When Jazz Was Invented*, a show that will rewrite the origin story of blues and jazz to include Southeastern Native peoples' music. She holds the John C. Hodges Chair of Excellence at the University of Tennessee in Knoxville.

ROLLAND (ROLLY) MEINHOLTZ has been a theater artist and educator for more than three decades. He holds theater degrees from Northwestern University and the University of Washington. Active as an actor, director, and playwright, he was the drama instructor at the Institute of American Indian Arts (IAIA), Santa Fe, New Mexico, 1964–1970. Working with students there, he created plays and theater events that arose directly out of the history and culture of Native Americans. They performed plays and toured nationally. Meinholtz was the artistic director of both the First and Second Festivals of Indian Performing Arts, sponsored by the Interior Department and presented in Washington, DC, 1965 and 1966. In 1970, Meinholtz joined the faculty of the theater department at the University of Montana. He was head of the directing program until 1992. Students of his have since formed the core of theater artists creating Native American theater today. These include poet Joy Harjo, playwright Bill Yellow Robe, actress Jane Lind, children's theater entrepreneur James Caron, educator and movement pioneer Charlie Oates, performance artist and monologist Moira O'Keefe, choreographer and actress Mary Kate Harris, and Arnie Fishbaugh, beloved and stunningly productive director of the Montana Council. Now retired, Meinholtz resides in Missoula with his wife Peggy, who is an actress and puppeteer.

MARY KATHRYN NAGLE is an enrolled citizen of the Cherokee Nation. She currently serves as executive director of the Yale Indigenous Performing Arts Program. She is also a partner at Pipestem Law, PC, where she works to protect tribal sovereignty and the inherent right of Indian Nations to protect their women and children from domestic violence and sexual assault. Nagle has authored numerous briefs in federal appellate courts, including the United States Supreme Court. Nagle studied theater and social justice at Georgetown University as an undergraduate student, and received her JD from Tulane University Law School, where she graduated summa cum laude and received the John Minor Wisdom Award. She is a frequent speaker at law schools and symposia across the country. Her articles have been published in law review journals including the *Harvard Journal of Law and Gender*, *Yale Law Journal* (online forum), *Tulsa Law Review*, and *Tulane Law Review*, among others.

Nagle is an alum of the 2012 Public Theater Emerging Writers Group, where she developed her play *Manahatta* in Public Studio (May 2014). Productions include *Miss Lead* (Amerinda, 59E59, January 2014) and *Fairly Traceable* (Native Voices at the Autry, March 2017). Recent productions include Arena Stage's world premiere of *Sovereignty*, and Oregon Shakespeare Festival's world premiere of *Manahatta*. In 2019, the Rose Theater (Omaha, Nebraska) will produce her new play *Return to Niobrara*.

Nagle has received commissions from Arena Stage (*Sovereignty*), the Rose Theater (*Return to Niobrara*), Portland Center Stage (*Mnisose*), Denver Center for the Performing Arts, and Yale Repertory Theatre.

The contributing co-editor, PRISCILLA PAGE, is a writer and dramaturg as well as a member of the dramaturgy faculty in the Department of Theater at the University of Massachusetts–Amherst, where she also serves as the director for the Multicultural Theater Certificate. Her research centers on Latina/o/x theater and contemporary Native American performance, and she is currently writing about Latina/o/x theater history in Chicago. She is a member of the Latinx Theater Commons, the Network of Ensemble Theaters, and Literary Managers and Dramaturgs of America (LMDA). She holds a BA in theater from California State University–East Bay, the state school where she grew up; an MFA in dramaturgy from the University of Massachusetts–Amherst; as well as a PhD in English, American Studies concentration, also from UMass–Amherst. Page served as the program curator for New WORLD Theater, a professional, nonprofit multicultural theater in residence at UMass Amherst, for five years.

Page's producing and dramaturgy credits include *Collidescope 2.0: Adventures in Pre and Post Racial America*, co-written and co-directed by Talvin Wilks and Ping Chong; *My Bronx*, written and performed by Terry Jenoure; *sash & trim*, written and performed by Djola Branner and directed by Laurie Carlos; *Crossing the Waters, Changing the Air*, written and directed by Ingrid Askew; and *Lydia on the Top Floor*, also written and performed by Terry Jenoure, and directed by Linda McInerney; and *Pelaje* by Migdalia Cruz, presented at Ateneo Puertorriqueño in San Juan, Puerto Rico. Her essay "My World Made Real" is published in Cruz's anthology *El Grito Del Bronx* (No PassPort Press, 2010).

RANDY REINHOLZ, an enrolled member of the Choctaw Nation of Oklahoma, was born in St. Louis, Missouri, and lived in several small towns throughout the US Midwest, in Missouri, North Dakota, and Texas. He graduated from high school in Camdenton, Missouri, and pursued a higher education afterward. He received his BA in communication from William Jewell College in 1984 and MFA in acting from Cornell University in 1988. He is the producing artistic director of Native Voices at the Autry, the nation's only Equity theater company dedicated exclusively to the development and production of new plays by Native American, First Nations, and Alaska Native playwrights, co-founded with producing executive director Jean Bruce Scott in 1993. They were honored for this work by Playwrights' Arena with the Lee Melville Award for Outstanding Contribution to the Los Angeles Theatre Community in 2015. *Off the Rails*, his bawdy and irreverent adaptation of Shakespeare's *Measure for Measure*, was developed by Native Voices at the Autry; it had its first production in Los Angeles in February 2015 and its world premiere at the Oregon Shakespeare Festival with Bill Rauch directing in July 2017. Reinholz wrote "Up from Violence and Empire" for American Theatre's "20 Years on Wilson's 'Ground': Voices Considering the Impact and the Lasting Legacy of August Wilson's Seminal 1995 Speech," and was honored as a Legacy Leader of Color for TCG's "The Ground at 20" video project. He has received a McKnight Fellowship and a MAP Grant. He has produced more than thirty scripts by Native American playwrights and directed over sixty plays in the United States, Australia, Mexico, and Canada, including *The Rez Sisters*; *Urban Tattoo*; *Jump Kiss*; *Now Look What You Made Me Do*; *The Waiting Room*; *How I Learned to Drive*; *Madame Mao*; *Blood at the Root*; *Anonymous*; *Wings of Night Sky, Wings of Morning Light*; *The Red Road*; and many productions of Shakespeare, Chekhov, and Ibsen plays. He is a tenured professor at San Diego State University, where he served as head of acting from 1997–2007, director of the School of Theatre, Television, and Film from 2007–2012, and director of community engagement and innovation for the College of Professional Studies and Fine Arts at SDSU from 2012–2015.